media

MANUAL

an introduction to SNG and ENG microwave

media

MANUAL

media

MANUAL

an introduction to SNG and ENG microwave

Jonathan Higgins

ELSEVIER

AMSTERDAM • BOSTON • HEIDELBERG • LONDON • NEW YORK • OXFORD
PARIS • SAN DIEGO • SAN FRANCISCO • SINGAPORE • SYDNEY • TOKYO
Focal Press is an imprint of Elsevier

Focal
Press

Elsevier Focal Press
Linacre House, Jordan Hill, Oxford OX2 8DP
200 Wheeler Road, Burlington MA 01803

First published 2004

British Library Cataloguing in Publication Data
A catalogue record for this book is available from the British Library

Library of Congress Cataloguing in Publication Data
Higgins, Jonathan.
  An introduction to SNG and ENG microwave/Jonathan Higgins.
    p.   cm. — (Media manual)
  1. Direct broadcast satellite television.   2. Microwave Communication
  systems.   3. Electronic news gathering.   I. Title.   II. Media manual.
  TK6677.H54 2003
  621.382—dc22

ISBN 0 240 51662 1

For information on all Focal Press publications visit our website at
www.focalpress.com

Typeset by Integra Software Services Pvt. Ltd, Pondicherry, India

Transferred to digital printing in 2008.

Contents

Acknowledgements

I am indebted to numerous colleagues and companies who have spent the time providing information for this book. In particular I would like to thank Mark Bell, crusader for ENG microwave safety; Richard Wolf and Mark Leonard of Wolf Coach; Peter Ward, series editor of the Media Manuals for his encouragement; and Christina Donaldson at Focal Press, who stoically accepted my excuses as several deadlines came and went.

I pay tribute to all the operators in the field around the world who use ENG and SNG links to deliver the stories for daily consumption by an audience who rarely hear about their activity behind the cameras, or appreciate the level of skill and professionalism that enables the coverage of these stories.

It is not always realised that sometimes these people risk too much for the sake of the story.

Not least, thanks to Annie for putting up with the burden of writing another book, and always being supportive and encouraging.

Jonathan Higgins

Introduction

Watch a TV news or sports programme anywhere in the world at any time, and it is highly likely that some (or all) of the events being televised will have been relayed back to the studio by the use of microwave communications at some point. The technology used to do this is highly complex, but the aim of this book is to cover the basics, giving you enough information to understand how, why and where these processes are used.

Microwave communications literally form a link in the chain of covering an event (and are so actually referred to as 'links'), and are a means to deliver TV signals back to the studio – a tool to get the job done.

Although we will primarily look at the use of microwave technology in an electronic news environment (with a particular focus on 'live' operations), we will also cover the differences when it is used in a sports or events situation – usually considered an outside broadcast (OB). We will talk about terrestrial microwave links and satellite links.

Both are essentially the same – with terrestrial microwave we are transmitting a microwave signal from one point directly to another point, a relatively short distance away on the Earth's surface, while with the satellite link we are transmitting a microwave signal up to a satellite, which then instantaneously re-transmits the microwave signal back down to the Earth.

It is important to note that with both of these, we are dealing with a microwave signal – the only significant difference is the length of path it takes and the direction it is pointed (ignoring some other differences that we will cover later).

With the satellite signal, the actual distance that the signal is connected between points on the Earth's surface could be 10 m or 10 000 km – a satellite signal's range is far greater than the terrestrial microwave link, which might typically connect only between 50 m and 80 km.

However, irrespective of the direct line distance across the Earth's surface, the distance the satellite signal has actually travelled will be around 70 000 km – the approximate round trip distance up to the satellite and back to wherever you are on the Earth's surface within the 'sight' of the satellite.

Over the years, there have been various definitions of electronic newsgathering (ENG) and OB, and the various operations that have been ascribed to either ENG or OB, and we will clarify what is generally understood by these terms across the industry.

We will look at the differences as well as the advantages and disadvantages of each type of signal transmission.

Hopefully, by the time you have finished reading this book, you will know which tool to use effectively in a particular situation, and why it is the right one to use.

Basic overview of the role of ENG/SNG

Television newsgathering is the process by which materials, i.e. pictures and sound, that help tell a story about a particular event are acquired and sent back to the studio. On arrival, they may be either relayed directly live to the viewer, or edited (packaged) for later transmission.

The process of newsgathering is a complex one, typically involving a cameraman and a reporter, a means of delivering the story back to the studio, and for live coverage, voice communication from the studio back to the reporter at the scene of the story.

Coverage of a sports event involves essentially the same elements but on a much greater scale. Instead of a single reporter you would have a number of commentators, and instead of a single cameraman, you might have up to thirty or forty cameras covering a major international golf tournament.

Whether it is a news or a sports event, the pictures and sound have to be sent back. This could be done by simply recording the coverage onto tape, and then taking it back to the studio. However, because of the need for immediacy, it is far more usual to send the coverage back by using a satellite or terrestrial microwave link, or via a fibre optic connection provided by, say, the telephone company. Plainly, here we are going to focus on the use of satellite and terrestrial microwave links.

A brief history

Some countries had TV services running in a rudimentary form before the outbreak of the Second World War in 1939, but it was only with the continued development of TV after war ended in 1945 that the use of microwave communications evolved. TV pictures from outside the studio were, by and large, originated using film cameras, and the film was brought back to the studio for processing and conversion to a TV picture.

Live coverage was very rare, as although electronic studio cameras could be used to transmit pictures over cable circuits provided by the telephone companies, this was only done for especially important events such as national political elections in the United States, and most notably, the Coronation of Queen Elizabeth II in the United Kingdom.

Up until the 1970s, 16 mm film was the common means of recording events on location for TV. By 1980, portable electronic cameras and video tape recorders (VTRs) developed in Japan and the United States began to feature in newsgathering, making it 'electronic' newsgathering (ENG), and by 1990 one-piece electronic camcorders were in common use. Within a decade, the use of film in TV for event coverage virtually disappeared. As a direct result of radar technology invented during the Second World War, microwave transmitters and receivers were developed and used from the 1950s onwards in the TV industry to transmit pictures and sound from point-to-point.

However, this early transmission equipment was bulky and not particularly reliable, but the development of solid-state electronics (as opposed to the use of vacuum tubes – 'valves') through the 1960s established terrestrial micro-wave link technology for coverage of remote events.

The use of satellite technology began in the late 1970s in the United States, with the development of transportable satellite earth stations (TES) which could be carried on the back of a truck. TV companies had to buy time on the satellites by the minute, and at the time this was particularly expensive – but as we shall see later, well worth it if it means it is the only way an event or story can be covered.

Through the 1980s TES (also called 'uplinks') were developed into both truck-based and flyaway forms. A flyaway is an uplink system comprised of boxed units that can be relatively easily transported by air if necessary.

In the 1990s, the use of digital compression developed, which both reduced the size and cost of these transportable systems and enabled broadcasters to use cheaper satellite capacity.

So the use of microwave links evolved from the 1950s through to the 1980s when ENG really came into its own. From the mid-1980s, the use of satellites to cover news and sports events developed to the extent that by the late 1990s, the use of terrestrial microwave for ENG became virtually limited to short-range local coverage of events.

As we shall see later, the development of digital transmission techniques has also breathed new life into the use of terrestrial ENG microwave – termed digital ENG (DENG).

Basic overview of the role of ENG/SNG

Definitions

ENG

Electronic newsgathering (ENG) is the term for collection of TV news stories using small hand-held electronic colour cameras, which may be used with microwave links, to deliver pictures and sound back to the studio and/or record the material locally on built-in recorders on the camera back. It therefore describes the use of electronic broadcasting equipment (as opposed to film equipment) to cover stories and events.

It has become a generic term and is not merely limited in its application to news, but in general refers to the use of camcorders as well as highly portable microwave and satellite equipment in the coverage of any televised event – be it news, sport or a spectacular. Typically the microwave-transmitting equipment is mounted in a van or truck, and ENG microwave trucks typically have a 'pump-up' mast that extends from 10 to 17 m, with a microwave transmitter and an antenna at the top.

OB

Outside broadcasting is the term for temporary provision of programme making facilities at the location of on-going news, sport or other events, lasting from a day to several weeks.

Outside broadcasts are generally planned in advance, but it is often necessary to accommodate short notice changes of venue or unforeseen requirements.

Microwave links may be required as a temporary point-to-point connection between the OB and the studio, as well as for portable links and wireless cameras on-site at the OB location. The definitions are not mutually exclusive, and certain operations could equally fit well into either or both categories. Added to this potential confusion is the fact that equipment manufacturers, in line with the terminology used in the United States, refer to everything as ENG.

It is not easy to discriminate between ENG and OB without ambiguity. Therefore for the purposes of this book, to avoid confusion, operations in terms of links considered under ENG can apply to OBs as well.

SNG

Satellite newsgathering (SNG) has become a generic term applied to any transportable satellite-transmitting earth station equipment used for the coverage of news, sports, or events.

Fundamentally, SNG describes the means by which material is gathered for TV broadcast and sent back to the studio using one (or more) satellites.

Typically the satellite-transmitting equipment is mounted in a truck, or packed and transported in cases (termed a flyaway). SNG trucks generally have a roof-mounted transmitting antenna.

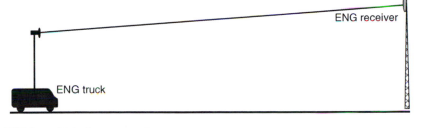

ENG receiver

ENG truck

ENG terrestrial microwave path

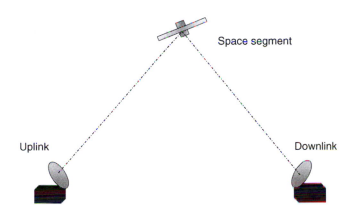

Space segment

Uplink

Downlink

Basic satellite path

Principal elements in covering an event

Let us just look at the principal elements of covering a news story from where it happens on location to its transmission from the TV studio.

We will pick a type of story that is of local and possibly national interest. Just suppose the story is the shooting of a police officer during a car chase following an armed robbery.

Camera and sound

The shooting happened around 2.30 pm, and the TV station newsroom was tipped off shortly after by a phone call from a member of the public at the scene.

Having checked the truth of the story with the police press office, by 3.00 pm the newsroom at the TV station despatched a cameraman (generically applied to both male and female camera operators) and a reporter to the location.

Generally these days, the cameraman is responsible for both shooting the pictures and recording the sound. The reporter finds out all the information on the circumstances of the armed robbery, the car chase and the shooting of the police officer. The cameraman may be shooting 'GVs' – general views of the scene and its surroundings onto tape – or interviews between the reporter, police spokesmen and eyewitnesses.

The reporter then will typically record a piece-to-camera (PTC), as shown in the following figure, which is where the reporter stands at a strategic point against a background which sets the scene for the story – perhaps the location where the officer was shot, the police station, or the hospital where the officer has been taken – and recounts the events, speaking and looking directly into the camera.

So by 5.00 pm the cameraman has several tapes (termed 'rushes'), showing the scene, interviews and the reporter's PTC. Now, will this material be edited on site to present the story, or will the rushes be sent directly back to the station to be edited ready for the studio to use in the 6.00 pm bulletin?

Editing

The 'cutting together' of the pictures and sound to form a 'cut-piece' or 'package' used to be carried out mostly back at the studio.

Mobile edit vehicles were usually only deployed on the 'big stories', or where there was editorial pressure to produce a cut-piece actually in the field. In the latter part of the 1990s, with the increasing use of the compact digital tape formats, the major manufacturers introduced laptop editors.

The laptop editor has both a tape player and a recorder integrated into one unit, with two small TV screens and a control panel. These units, which are slightly larger and heavier than a laptop computer, can be used either by a picture editor, or more commonly nowadays, by the cameraman.

During the 1990s, the pressure on TV organisations to reduce costs led to the introduction of multi-skilling, where technicians, operators and journalists are trained in at least one (and often two) other crafts apart from their primary core skill.

Piece-to-camera (© Telecast Fiber Inc.)

However, the production of a news story is rarely a contiguous serial process – more commonly, several tasks need to be carried out in parallel. For instance, the main package may need to be begun to be edited while the cameraman has to go off and shoot some extra material.

The combination of skills can be quite intriguing, so we can have a cameraman who can record sound and edit tape; a reporter who can also edit tape and/or shoot video and record sound (often referred to as a video journalist or VJ); or a microwave technician who can operate a camera and edit.

So it is often a juggling act to make sure that the right number of people with the right combination of skills available are on location all at the same time.

Getting the story back

There are now three options as to how we get the story back to the studio for transmission on the 6 o'clock news bulletin – it can be:

- taken back in person by the reporter and/or the cameraman
- sent back via motorbike despatch rider
- transmitted from an ENG microwave or SNG microwave truck.

The first two are obvious and so we need not concern ourselves any further. The third option is of course what we are focussed on – and in any case, is the norm nowadays for sending material in this type of situation from location back to the studio.

As it turns out, the newsdesk – realizing the scale of the story once the reporter was on the scene – had despatched a microwave truck down to the location at 4.00 pm. The ENG microwave or SNG truck (for our purposes here it does not matter which) finds a suitable position, and establishes a link back to the studio, with both programme and technical communications in place.

By just gone 5.00 pm, the tape material (rushes or edited package) is replayed from the VTR in the truck back to the studio.

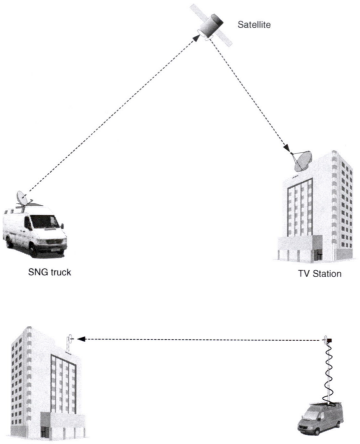

Getting the story back

Going live

The reporter may actually have to do a 'live' report back to the studio during the news bulletin, and this is accomplished by connecting the camera to the microwave link truck (along with sound signal from the reporter's microphone) either via a cable, a fibre optic connection or using a short-range microwave link (more on that later).

From the studio, a 'feed' of the studio presenter's microphone is radioed back to the truck, and fed into an earpiece in the reporter's ear, so that the studio presenter can ask the reporter questions about the latest on the situation. The reporter will also be provided with a small picture monitor (out of camera shot) so that they can see an 'off-air' feed of the bulletin.

This is commonly known as a 'live two-way', and what the viewer sees is a presentation of the story, switching between the studio and the location. We will look at this process in more detail in a moment.

Reporter going live

Typical transmission chain

We now have all the elements that form the transmission chain between the location and the studio, enabling either taped or live material to be transmitted.

The camera and microphone capture the pictures and sound. The material is then perhaps edited on site, and then the pictures and sound – whether rushes, edited or 'live' – are sent back via the truck (ENG microwave or SNG) to the TV station.

The processes that occur at either end of the chain are the same no matter whether the signals are sent back via terrestrial microwave or via satellite.

Communication with the studio

Being able to keep constantly in touch with both the newsroom and the studio is absolutely vital to a successful transmission. This is true during both the preparation of the story and the actual transmission – particularly if it is to be 'live'.

Typically the primary communication with the reporter, cameraman and SNG/ENG truck operator is via cellphone and pager. All these key personnel typically carry both a pager and a cellphone.

This might seem somewhat over-cautious, but you should always be aware that cellphones may not work in certain areas for a number of reasons – screening from being within a building, network congestion or just generally poor coverage.

However, pagers, principally because they operate at a much lower frequency, do not suffer from these problems. All the key people on location must be able at least to receive important messages from the TV station, and be able to respond – even if it means stopping at a public payphone to do so!

For live transmissions, another layer of communication (commonly termed 'comms') is required – that of the studio control room being able to route communications related to the programme to and from the reporter and crew at the scene.

The 'live' crew on location must be able to hear what is going on in both the studio control room (sometimes referred to as the 'gallery') and the studio itself.

Talkback
The circuit that carries purely technical conversations is typically known as talkback, and there is ideally both talkback from the studio gallery to the truck, and a reverse talkback from the truck to the studio.

These circuits together are often referred to as a '4-wire', from the property of having a separate send and return circuits enabling simultaneous bidirectional (two-way) conversations.

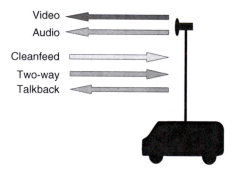

Typical signals to/from newsgathering vehicle

The circuit which carries the studio programme output is vital, as the reporter must be able to hear the studio presenter to introduce or link into the live piece, listen to cues from the studio control room, and also be able to conduct a two-way dialogue with the studio presenter, which requires the reporter to hear the questions from the studio.

The feed of the studio output to the location is known by a number of names, and the usage vary slightly – cleanfeed, mix-minus, reverse audio, return audio or interrupted fold back (IFB) – so what is actually carried on this the circuit varies slightly according to the term.

Mix-Minus

Cleanfeed, mix-minus, reverse audio and return audio are all terms for what is essentially the same thing – a mix of the studio output without the audio contribution from the remote location. This is important, because if the reporter just listened to the straight output of the studio 'off-air', the reporter's own voice would in effect be heard transmitted to the studio, and then sent back to the location.

The reporter would then hear his/her voice slightly delayed as an echo in their earpiece, which is very off-putting. It is therefore very important that the reporter hears everything being transmitted from the studio 'less' (without) his/her own voice – hence the technically accurate term 'mix-minus'.

IFB is this same mix, but with talkback from the studio gallery superimposed on top. Switched talkback can sometimes be superimposed on the cleanfeed type of circuit as well. The exact configuration varies from broadcaster to broadcaster, and local variations are common.

The reporter, with an earpiece, and the cameraman with either an earpiece or headphones, will be connected to the truck listening to the studio circuit, and this connection will use cable or wireless belt-pack receivers.

These belt-pack receivers pick up the studio comms circuit via a small localized transmitter on the truck. Later on we will see how these circuits can be established – there are a number of ways of doing so.

Back to the story

But for the time being let us just return to our police shooting story outside the hospital where the injured officer is being treated, and look at the process of going live in a little more detail.

The studio has asked for a 'live' from the hospital where the police officer is being treated at around 6.05 pm (it is an important story, so it is near the top of the running order of the news bulletin), and it is going to last for around 2 minutes. As we said earlier, the reporter stands in front of the camera, with an earpiece that has a cleanfeed mix from the studio.

The cameraman will also have an earpiece fed with the same as the reporter, as it is just as important that he/she knows exactly what is going on, and these feeds are connected through the truck.

The operator in the truck will also be able to both listen to what is coming from the studio in terms of both cleanfeed and talkback, and also be able to speak to both the cameraman and the reporter via their earpieces.

Let us suppose that the team have already edited and fed a cut-piece back to the studio, which shows the scene of the shooting, and some eyewitness interviews – and this lasts for around 2 minutes.

At 6.04 pm, the studio presenter first introduces the story, summarizing the events so far, and then introduces the cut-piece – this is usually played out from the studio (unless it was only finished close to the 'live', and then it may be played out from the truck).

Outside the hospital, the truck operator, the cameraman and the reporter can also hear all of this. It is highly desirable for the truck operator to have got a feed of the 'off-air' TV signal, and fed only the off-air video to the camera position where the reporter can see it in his/her field of view on a video monitor without having to avert their eyes obviously from the camera.

As the reporter can see and hear the cut-piece, and because the reporter wrote and recorded the script for the cut-piece earlier, he/she will (hopefully!) know what the concluding sentence is (commonly referred to as the 'out-words').

During all of this, the truck operator will have been confirming to the studio that they are ready to 'go live', and that the video and audio levels from the truck have been checked and are correct. The truck operator will also make a last minute check with both the cameraman and the reporter that they can hear everything clearly.

At the end of the edited cut-piece (we are now at 6.06 pm), the studio output switches from the tape back to the studio presenter who then introduces the reporter, and the studio 'cuts' seamlessly from the studio presenter to the reporter outside the hospital.

At this point, the cleanfeed from the studio will go dead in the reporter's ear, so that he/she can then speak without hearing themselves back as an annoying echo as we mentioned earlier. As soon as the reporter finishes speaking, their earpiece will spring into life with another question from the studio presenter, and the reporter replies, etc.

This will continue for a period of around 2 minutes, as agreed previously with the studio. As the end time approaches, on the talkback circuit the studio calls out '10 seconds'...'5 seconds'...and hearing this countdown, the reporter smoothly finishes and 'hands back' to the studio – it is now 6.08 pm.

As soon as the studio has moved on into the next item in the bulletin, they will call a 'clear' on the talkback circuit, and everyone can relax – and I do mean relax! The process of going live is very stressful for everyone – it does not matter how large or small the audience.

There is great emphasis on timing and 'getting it right', and the 'post-mortems' that occur when it does not go right, even in way that the viewer at home would barely notice (if at all), often defies belief – remember no one dies because of television!

It is very important to look smooth and slick in presentation, and the pressure on the reporter, the cameraman and the microwave technician to deliver the live report of a programme may seem out of proportion (after all, no one dies because of TV – but trying telling that to the news editor!). There is a commonly held fear that peoples' careers are 'on the line' in live broadcasting.

On a story like this, which would generally have a high 'newsworthy' value, the crew are likely to have to stay at the location to provide updates on the situation.

Particularly with advent of 24-hour news channels – which have a notoriously voracious appetite for news material – the truck and crew could remain on 'stake-out' for some considerable time, and have to provide a number of 'live updates' through the evening – even if there is nothing to say!

You should now have an overall appreciation of what is involved in undertaking coverage of a news story, and we have looked at the mechanics of what happens at the 'live end' in covering this story – and we will come back to this story a little later.

Principal elements in covering an event

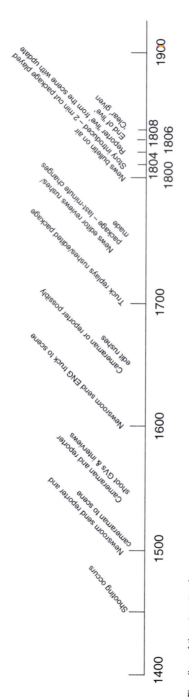

Shooting occurs

Newsroom send reporter and cameraman to scene

Cameraman and reporter shoot GVs & interviews

Newsroom send ENG truck to scene

Cameraman or reporter possibly edit rushes

Truck relays rushes/edited package

News editor reviews rushes/ package – last-minute changes made

News bulletin on air
Story introduced – 2 min cut package played
Reporter 'live' from the scene with update
End of 'live', 'Clear' given

1400 1500 1600 1700 1800 1804 1806 1808 1900

Timeline of the story to air

Analogue theory

In telecommunications, the resource of electromagnetic spectrum – which is the basis of telecommunications – is commonly referred to as RF – an acronym for radio frequency. In our context, it does not refer to media such as radio stations and their broadcasts, but refers to the term used in the scientific sense, as defined in the dictionary, as 'rays' or 'radiation'.

This can be confusing for non-scientists, but is in fact the original definition of radio. It has also been historically referred to as 'airwaves', or as the 'ether', and a specific frequency in the spectrum can be referred to as a 'wavelength'. All these terms refer to electromagnetic spectrum.

Many of you will have heard of technologies associated with the word digital, and perhaps also heard reference to the word 'analogue' (usually associated mistakenly with old-fashioned) – but what do they mean?

Analogue basics

All forms of electromagnetic radiation (including light) can be thought of as consisting of waves. In electronics, an analogue signal is a wave signal that carries information by the continuous varying of its amplitude (size) and frequency (period) as shown in the diagram.

The concept is comparable to two people, each holding the end of a rope and standing some distance apart.

One person acts as the 'transmitter' and one as the 'receiver'. The 'transmitter' flicks the end of the rope up and down, creating a wave shape that passes down the rope to the 'receiver'.

The harder the rope is flicked, the greater the amplitude of the wave, and the more frequently it is flicked, the faster the waves are created and the faster the rope oscillates.

This demonstrates the two fundamental properties of an analogue signal – amplitude and frequency. One complete wave is equal to 1 cycle or 1 Hertz (Hz).

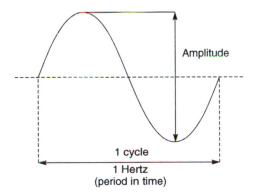

Analogue wave cycle

This is how many electrical signals are conveyed, such as those reproduced by hi-fi systems. In terms of audio, the amplitude is the volume or 'loudness', and the period is the frequency or 'pitch' of the audio signal.

The human ear is sensitive to a frequency range of approximately 50–20 000 Hz (20 kHz), and so, loud, high-pitched sound signals correspond to large and closely spaced waves, and quiet low-pitched signals to small and widely spaced waves.

Obviously, these elements vary independently to create the spectrum of the typical audio programme sound.

Frequency and wavelength

When we talk of the frequencies used for transmitting video and audio, we refer to signals as radio frequencies (RF), but this is not strictly limited to the relatively narrow band of frequencies that we listen to radio broadcasts on. It also refers to a very wide range of frequencies that encompass microwaves as well.

Historically, frequencies were measured in terms of the distance (in metres) between the peaks of two consecutive cycles of a radio wave – wavelength – instead of the number of cycles per second or Hertz.

Even though radio waves are at a very high frequency, there is a tiny (but measurable) distance between the cycles of electromagnetic waves. This corresponds to the distance light would travel, as electromagnetic waves travel at the speed of light – 300 000 km per second.

As we characterize electromagnetic waves by their wavelength, radio waves have much shorter wavelengths and therefore higher frequencies than audio signals.

Order of magnitude		Notation
1		1 Hz
100		100 Hz (0.1 kHz)
1000	thousand – kilo	1 kHz
1 000 000	million – mega	1 MHz
1 000 000 000	thousand million – giga	1 GHz

But comparing with further up the electromagnetic spectrum, radio waves have much longer wavelengths and thus lower frequencies than visible light waves.

However, when sending video and audio via a radio signal, just transmitting pure wave signals is not enough if we want to convey such complex information as pictures and sound. We need to superimpose the information onto the pure wave signal, using a process called 'modulation' – we will look at this further in a while.

Phase

An electromagnetic wave signal also possesses the property of 'phase', and a complete cycle can be said to equal to 360° (as in a circle). Looking at our wave signal from just now, let us compare it with an identical signal alongside it.

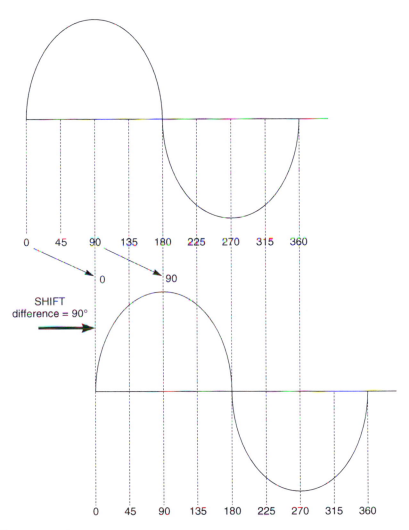

Phase comparison

If the two signals are exactly coincident, i.e. the peaks and troughs occur at exactly the same time, they are said to be 'in phase'. If there is a difference (as shown in the lower part of the diagram), then there is a phase difference and the signals are said to be 'out of phase' relative to each other.

A practical example of the out-of-phase condition is when you wire the speakers up on your hi-fi, but reversing one speaker's positive and negative connections. When you feed music via the amplifier to the speakers, then as one speaker cone moves in and out reproducing the music, the other speaker cone is moving in the opposing direction, counteracting the sound pressure waves from the other speaker. The result is that the sound waves in the room tend to almost cancel out, and you end up with a rather thin reedy sound. There is no damage done to the speakers (unless you turn them up really loud!) but the phase cancellation will completely spoil the music.

The property of phase is important in microwave and satellite communications, and particularly when we look at some types of modulation.

Modulation principles

Our video or audio signal is a message or information signal. A radio transmitter is a device that converts this type of message signal (often termed the baseband signal), to a signal at a much higher frequency and power that can travel over a distance (often termed the carrier signal). Although it is at a much higher frequency, the amplitude and the frequency of the original signal can be received at a distant point. The process of preparing this transmitted signal, which is a mixture of the information and a carrier signal, is called 'modulation'. The opposite process of recreating the original baseband information signal is called 'demodulation'.

There are a number of different types of modulation, but analogue modulation techniques generally fall under either amplitude modulation (AM) or frequency modulation (FM).

AM

Amplitude modulation is a process where a baseband message signal modulates (alters) the amplitude and frequency of a high frequency carrier signal that is at a nominally fixed frequency, so that the carrier signal varies in amplitude and frequency in concert with the baseband signal. The intensity, or amplitude, of the carrier wave varies in accordance with the modulating signal, and a fraction of the power is converted to 'sidebands' extending above and below the carrier frequency.

If this signal is analysed, it can be seen to contain the original carrier signal plus these lower and upper sidebands of frequencies. The entire modulated carrier now occupies a frequency range termed the RF bandwidth. However, this form of modulation is not an efficient way to send information, particularly for our purposes – we have just described it here for illustrative purposes so that you get the idea.

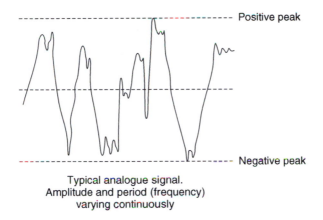

--- Positive peak

--- Negative peak

Typical analogue signal.
Amplitude and period (frequency)
varying continuously

AM

FM

Frequency modulation is of more interest as it is used for analogue transmissions in particularly analogue terrestrial microwave. The principle of FM is based on a carrier wave signal that shifts up and down in frequency (deviates) from its centre (at rest) frequency, in direct relationship to the amplitude of the baseband signal, though the amplitude remains at a constant level.

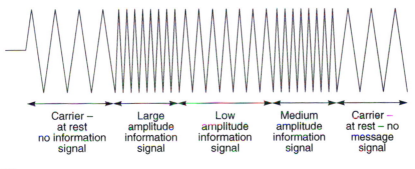

| Carrier –
at rest
no information
signal | Large
amplitude
information
signal | Low
amplitude
information
signal | Medium
amplitude
information
signal | Carrier –
at rest – no
message
signal |

FM

The maximum deviation (frequency shift) of the frequency is equal above and below the centre frequency, and is usually referred to as the peak-to-peak deviation.

In an FM signal, the instantaneous frequency of the baseband signal is represented by the instantaneous rate of change (speed of change) of the carrier frequency. If the modulated signal waveform is viewed on an electronic measurement instrument such as an oscilloscope or a spectrum analyser, the relationship appears much more complex than in AM, and it is difficult to see exactly what is occurring.

The advantage of FM is that the signal has significantly greater protection from random effects (termed noise) than AM, and is much more effective than AM at very high carrier frequencies used for satellite transmissions. FM is spectrally very inefficient, i.e. the amount of bandwidth required to transmit a message signal is greater, but if the right conditions are met, it produces a much higher quality signal compared to AM. The concept of FM is quite a difficult one to grasp, but it is important to understand that for our purposes it is an efficient way of transmitting information.

The TV picture

When you sit in your living room, watching TV, have you ever wondered how the picture is made up? If you are reading this book, the answer is probably 'yes'.

How can we send a moving picture down a cable or over the air? Well, we have to break it up into pieces. Think of each picture you see on the screen at any one instant as a frame – like a single slide in a slide show – and TV is just a very fast slide show. Within each frame of the TV picture, there are areas of different brightness (luminance) and colour (chrominance). We call the smallest perceptible block of picture a 'pixel' (an abbreviation of picture element).

Now we need to know which parts of the picture are bright and which bits are particular colours. So we divide the frame up into tiny horizontal strips referred to as lines, and so each frame of a TV picture is made up of 525 or 625 lines. The number of lines depends on the TV standard used in a particular country – so for example, it is 525 lines in United States and Japan, and 625 lines in Europe. In addition we need to define how many frames we are going to send each second, and that is either 25 or 30 fps (frames per second). In addition, the lines are 'interlaced' within frames – we will see how this works in a minute.

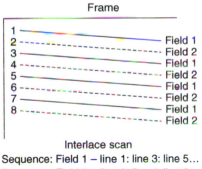

Interlace scan
Sequence: Field 1 – line 1: line 3: line 5...
Sequence: Field 2 – line 2: line 4: line 6...

Line and frame structure of TV picture

Colour information

Let us just briefly look at the way the luminance and chrominance information is conveyed to the brain. The eye registers the amount of light coming from a scene, and visible light is made up of differing amounts of the three primary colours of red, green and blue. In terms of TV, the colour white is made up of proportions of red (30%), green (59%) and blue (11%) signals.

As with many aspects of TV technology, the method of transmitting a colour signal is a compromise. Back in the 1950s and 1960s when colour TV was being introduced, both the American (NTSC) and European (PAL) colour systems had to be able to produce a satisfactory black and white signal on the existing monochrome TV sets. Therefore, both colour systems derive a composite luminance signal from 'matrixing' (mixing) the red, green and blue signals. The matrix circuitry also produces colour difference signals, which when transmitted are disregarded by the monochrome receivers, but form the colour components for colour TV receivers for re-matrixing with the luminance signal to reconstitute the original full colour picture.

Why produce colour difference signals? Why not simply transmit the red, green and blue signals individually? Well, this is a demonstration of the early use of compression in the analogue domain.

Individual chrominance signals would each require full bandwidth, and as a video signal requires around 5 MHz of bandwidth for reasonable sharpness, the three colour signals would require 15 MHz in total. The analogue TV signal that is transmitted to the viewer is termed 'composite', as it combines the luminance, colour and timing signals into one combined signal, and the technique of embedding the colour information as 'colour difference' in along with the luminance signal requires only 5.5 MHz of bandwidth.

Capitalizing on the brain's weaknesses

By relying on the relatively poor colour perception of the human brain, the colour signals can be reduced in bandwidth so that the entire luminance and chrominance signal fits into 5 MHz of bandwidth – a reduction of 3:1. This is achieved by the use of colour difference signals – known as the red difference signal and the blue difference signal – which are essentially signals representing the difference in brightness between the luminance and each colour signal.

The eye is more sensitive to changes in brightness than in colour, i.e. it can more easily see an error when a pixel is too bright or too dark, rather than if it has too much red or too much blue. What happened to the green signal, then? Well, if we have the luminance (which if you recall is made up of red, green and blue), and the red and blue difference signals, we can derive the green signal back from these three signals by a process of subtraction.

Frames

We now need to process each frame of the picture. In NTSC, there are 525 lines in every frame, and the frame rate is 30 fps; in PAL, there are 625 lines per frame, and the frame rate is 25 fps.

If a video frame is 'progressively' scanned, each line is scanned in sequence in the frame, and if this is done (as in PAL) 25 times per second, then a significant amount of bandwidth is required. If the frame is scanned in an interlaced structure, where each frame is divided into a pair of TV fields each sending odd- and then even-numbered lines in alternate sequence, then this both saves bandwidth and gives the appearance that the picture is 'refreshed' 50 times per second – which looks very smooth to the human eye, and the human brain quickly adapts. Thus, 25/30 frames per second are displayed as 50/60 fields per second with half the number of lines in each field.

Brightness = luminance
Colour = chrominance
Colour difference = luminance-red; luminance-blue
Two fields = one frame
625 or 525 = one frame

The TV picture

Digital

A digital signal conveys information as a series of 'on' and 'off' states, which can be thought of corresponding to numbers '1' and '0' – this is based on the binary number system.

In a stream of 1s and 0s, each 1 and each 0 is termed a bit, and a digital signal is defined by the parameter of bits. For instance, the signal is transmitted at a certain speed called the bit-rate, which is often measured in bits per second (bps). You may recognize this when looking at the modem speed on your computer, and how fast it can communicate over a telephone line.

The advantage of using the binary system of 1s and 0s is that these numbers are very easy to transmit electronically rapidly as 'on' and 'off'. Morse code is a similar type of system, where the message is conveyed by flashing a light on and off, or turning an audio tone on and off, in a coded sequence.

The analogue signal – and this can be either a video or audio signal – is converted to a digital signal by slicing or sampling the analogue signal thousands or millions of times per second. In effect sampling is taking a series of snapshots of the level of the analogue signal at each instant.

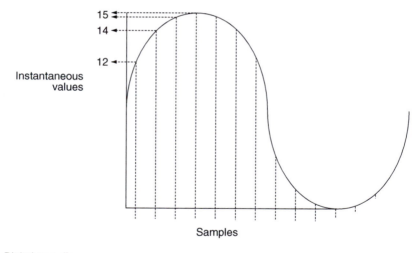

Digital sampling

Each sample value is then converted to a binary number and transmitted. At the receiving end, these numbers are converted back to ordinary numbers and by electronically 'joining the dots up', the original shape of the analogue signal can be reconstructed.

34

Joining the dots up

The advantage of a digital signal, particularly in relation to microwave trans-missions, is that the amount of power required to successfully transmit it can be significantly lower than the power required for analogue transmission.

This is because in general the signals are more easily recovered from the background interference 'noise'.

Phase modulation

We can also convey information by varying the phase of the carrier signal, and although it is used to in the analogue domain (particularly TV signals), it is important when we come to look at digital modulation.

Imagine we have two signals, identical in phase. If we move the second carrier signal (our information signal) forwards or backwards in phase relative to the first signal (which we can call the reference signal), we can convey information.

Now, you may say, that is not very efficient if we have to transmit two signals – but we do not actually transmit the reference signal – only one signal is transmitted. Instead, using some clever processing, we can recreate the reference signal from the carrier signal at the far end.

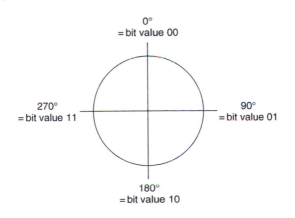

Using phase to convey information

Terrestrial microwave links

A microwave link fundamentally consists of a transmitter (often abbreviated to TX) and a receiver (RX). The transmitter and the receiver are each connected to an antenna. This is typically a parabolic dish antenna connected to the transmitter, and also typically a dish antenna at the receiver (though there are a few other specialized antenna types used with both the transmitter and the receiver).

The receiver needs to be typically within 65 km range of the transmitter – but this distance is very much dependent upon local obstructions and the geography of the land (the topography) on the path between the transmitter and the receiver. There are few hard and fast rules about what will and will not work, though the principal one is that if there is a large object in the path close to the transmitter, the link is unlikely to work.

Line of sight

In general, in order for microwave antennas to achieve clear transmission there must be an uninterrupted path between the transmitting antenna and the receiving antenna – termed 'line of sight'. The maximum operating distance across each country between a microwave transmitter and a receiver is dictated principally by the curvature of the earth. Although as we have just noted, generally for a microwave link to work there needs to be a clear line of sight between the transmitter and the receiver. There are some circumstances where this need not be the case, as we shall see later.

Because the earth's surface is curved, the effective distance between two points that can be seen is limited. If you stand at the seashore, in theory, on a clear day you can see to a distance of about 5 km to the level of the water at the horizon. If you were looking at say a ship on the horizon, you would be able to see it further – perhaps 15 km depending on the size of the ship – because of its height above the sea.

As we said earlier, ENG microwave trucks typically have a 'pump-up' mast that extends from 10 to 17 m, and this gives us a significant height advantage. If the receiver to which it is transmitting is perhaps 100 m high, then we can achieve a theoretical unobstructed distance of around 50 km.

Microwave frequencies

Microwave transmissions occupy the 2–50 GHz range of the electromagnetic spectrum. The higher the transmission frequency, for a given transmission power, the shorter the distance across which a reliable transmission can be achieved.

A microwave signal is characterized by the fact that it is at a very high frequency, and hence the wavelength (i.e. the distance between the peaks of the signal) is very small. In the frequency spectrum, microwaves sit some way above normal TV signals transmitted to the home, and below infrared radiation.

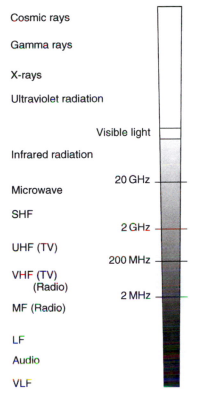

Cosmic rays

Gamma rays

X-rays

Ultraviolet radiation

Visible light

Infrared radiation

Microwave — 20 GHz

SHF

2 GHz

UHF (TV)

200 MHz

VHF (TV)
(Radio)

2 MHz

MF (Radio)

LF

Audio

VLF

Electromagnetic spectrum

Microwave frequency bands for ENG

Microwaves have properties similar to visible light. They travel in a straight line; they cannot pass through solid objects; but they can be reflected off flat or curved surfaces like light from a mirror. The range of microwave frequencies used for terrestrial ENG are typically in the 2–8 GHz band, though this band is not exclusively for ENG use, but is shared with other microwave services.

This frequency band is used because it has been allocated by the global body that decides on RF usage, the International Telecommunications Union (ITU).

In the United Kingdom, the 2 GHz ENG band is divided up into 12 channels, each 20 MHz wide, spanning 2.44–2.68 GHz. The 7 GHz band has 4 channels. Across Europe there are similar allocations.

In the United States, the 2 GHz broadcast auxiliary service (BAS) band consists of 7 primary channels in 120 MHz, with channel 1 being 18 MHz wide while channels 2 through 7 are 17 MHz wide. The 7 GHz BAS has 14 channels, each 25 MHz wide.

Terrestrial microwave links

There is therefore considerable pressure to share access to this relatively small number of channels in an equitable fashion.

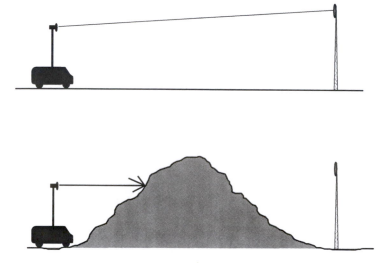

TX and RX – line of sight and obstructed

Microwave – and the microwave

At this point let us just mention the 'microwave' that you are undoubtedly more familiar with (and with which you may have been a little confused about in our discussion here) – the microwave oven found in every kitchen. A microwave oven works by generating an alternating power field that agitates water molecules, resulting in the generation of heat. Remembering that most organic matter (plants, meat – that includes people) are mostly made up of water molecules, the food is heated from the inside outwards, leaving the dishes and the oven itself cool, because they are not directly heated due to their different molecular structure compared to living matter.

By international standard, the frequency at which microwave ovens operate is 2.45 GHz, and hence it is in the frequency band we are discussing. Might this cause interference problems? No, because the electric field generated inside the oven is very much focussed on the centre of the oven, and at a relatively low power.

So could microwave-transmitting equipment cause safety problems in terms of heating people up – the answer is yes!

Later on we will look at these safety issues, as it is perfectly possible for microwave-transmitting equipment to cause internal body heating when it is used incorrectly or if there is a fault.

Fresnel zones

Water, in the form of humid air, fog or rain absorbs microwave energy and can disrupt transmissions. At the middle point between a transmitter and a receiver, the beam can spread in diameter up to tens of metres and this area, known as the Fresnel zone, must be completely clear of obstructions such as trees, buildings, or any area of ground such as hills. Fresnel zones are all about 'reflections'.

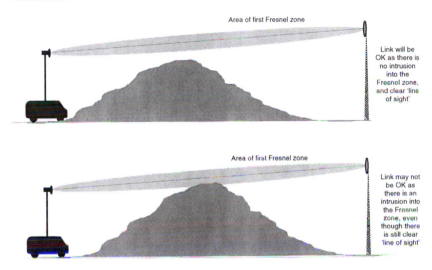

Fresnel zones

The mathematical theory surrounding Fresnel zones is very complex, and so we need to concern ourselves only with the area described as the first Fresnel zone. There should not be any obstruction within this area, as it is likely that a reflection will cause an 'opposing' signal to be bounced off the obstruction towards the receiver. When it arrives at the receiver, it would either add or subtract from the original direct (non-reflected) signal.

If the reflected radio wave is in phase with the direct signal then the reflection has an adding effect, and so improves the received signal. On the other hand, if the radio wave arrives out of phase relative to the direct signal, the reflection has a cancelling effect on the directly received signal.

This is known as multipath fading, and has at the very least a ghosting effect on pictures, which is seen as a one or more faint copies of the original image displaced to the left or right of the picture on the screen. At worst, it results in no signal being received at all.

These effects on the radio wave path are further complicated by the earth's curvature, which can affect the radio wave due to atmospheric anomalies such as ducting and layering.

39

During certain parts of the day and night the atmosphere causes the radio wave to 'bend' according to atmospheric conditions. You would have probably noticed that as the TV signal at home is affected by very hot conditions in the summer or very cold dry weather in winter, the microwave link can also be affected in the same way.

For temporary ENG links, this can give rise to unforeseen problems as there is rarely time to 'design' the link as you would do for a permanent installation, where you would carry out careful calculations relating to the topography and extremes of weather that might be suffered during the year.

Ghosting

Instead, it is all a matter of getting out to the location and getting pictures back. However, for a major event that is known about beforehand, it is possible to check link path performance.

You can do this in two ways. First, by use of specialized software tools, a path profile calculation can be performed. Such software packages have a database containing digitized map information.

The program creates a path profile from topographical map information in the database based on the location of the TX and RX points, which be translated into an elevation profile of the land between the two sites on the path – a cross-section of the land underneath the signal path.

Earth's curvature is calculated and added, as that of any known obstacles. The Fresnel zone calculation can then be applied and any potential clearance problems displayed.

Secondly (and often the easiest and certainly the most reliable), you can actually go out and perform a site test or site survey, using a microwave truck, from the event location back to the receiver.

This will give a very good measure as to whether the link for the event will work – except consideration must still be given as to whether the link path is likely to be affected on the day by weather conditions, or any local obstructions that may cause problems.

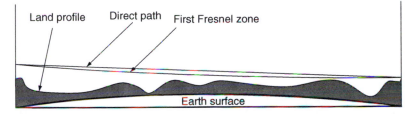

Typical path profile

For instance, are there trees within close distance to the transmitter, which may be in leaf when the event occurs? Links are rarely affected when 'shooting' through bare trees – but can be dramatically attenuated when trees are in leaf.

If the link path crosses tidal waters, it may be affected by the tides them-selves, and it has been known for a link to work in the morning when it is first set up, and successfully used for the lunchtime news bulletin – only for it to fail during the afternoon as the tide has come in or gone out!

The other factor that could be calculated is a link budget – which is often part of the software packages. However, these are rarely calculated for ENG microwave, and the principles of link budgets will be covered later when we look at SNG, where they are of more significance.

Fade margin

The difference between the operating level of the link and the point at which it fails, because the power level reaching the receiver is too low, is called the 'fade margin'. Normally, the fade margin will be set to overcome link impairments such as multipath, diffraction, refraction, polarization and absorption losses. We see the same term used in satellite links as well.

Fresnel zones

Digital modulation in ENG microwave

Earlier we discussed AM and FM, and as we saw, both are methods of transmitting information on a carrier wave radio signal. Both AM and FM are used in broadcasting radio and analogue TV. In the context of digital, a new method of modulation joins the fray – coded orthogonal frequency division multiplex (COFDM).

Like many of the subjects in this book, it is too complex a subject to cover in detail, so we will just look at the bare essentials.

COFDM

For COFDM to work, it is necessary for the information signal to undergo a process known as compression, but as it is common to satellite communications, we will look at how compression works in more detail later. So for the time being, assume our digital signal has been compressed.

Instead of using just a single information carrier, COFDM uses a large number of narrow information carriers – typically at least 2000 – each carrying a slice of the total compressed data.

The term 'orthogonality' comes from the property where the phase of one carrier is different from that of the carrier next to it. The demodulator for one carrier does not 'see' the modulation of the others, hence there is no crosstalk or interference between carriers, even though the signals overlap in frequency.

As each carrier has a low data rate in itself, i.e. the data is being transmitted at a low speed, the susceptibility to interference from multipath (ghosting) is greatly reduced, as any reflected signal will be detected at the same time as the direct signal – and in fact that additional reflected signal can enhance the direct signal.

This is because the period in which the data is received and decoded is lengthy compared with the time in which any delayed signals will arrive. It is also possible to enhance the multipath immunity by the addition of a 'guard interval', which is a space between each transmitted carrier.

So data is transmitted for a period that is longer than the time during which the receiver is detecting it. Also, the use of coding (the 'C' in COFDM) is another significant factor in coping with both interference between channels and the frequency-dependent fading caused by multipath.

To sum up, COFDM thrives in an environment where there are a lot of reflections, as these can actually enhance certain aspects of the received signal. However, although it seems to be an ideal step forward from analogue FM, there are certain limitations to its use, and there can be situations where analogue FM performs better.

At the time of writing, many are still exploring the use of COFDM for ENG/OB applications, and further development and refining will result.

Compression

If digital signals were used in direct replacement for the same analogue information, the resultant bit-rate at which the information would have to be transmitted would be very high.

This would use much more bandwidth (frequency spectrum) than an equivalent analogue transmission, and therefore is not very efficient.

There is a need to strip out the redundant and insignificant information in the signal, and this process of data rate reduction, or compression as it is more commonly referred to, is dealt with in more detail later.

The important point to grasp is that digital signals are now the norm particularly for SNG transmissions. In ENG microwave, analogue transmission is still the preferred method, but that is slowly changing with the new generation of digital ENG microwave equipment that has come onto the market.

Advantages of digital microwave

The spread in use of COFDM includes:

- traditional, van-based ENG
- dual-mode (hybrid) DSNG and ENG vehicles
- mobile news cars and sports utility vehicles
- airborne applications
- tripod portable applications.

Many broadcast operations have turned to DSNG trucks for covering events outside their primary market. Unfortunately, such trucks are often under utilized because they do not include terrestrial microwave systems for in-market applications. Often, DSNG trucks also cannot get a clean line of sight in urban concrete 'canyons', limiting their usefulness. By adding a low-profile omnidirectional antenna, and a COFDM modulator and transmitter, such vehicles can become cost-effective dual-mode (hybrid) trucks without the added weight, mass and cost of a hydraulic mast. We will examine hybrid trucks in more detail later. For new DSNG trucks, COFDM provides a low-cost way of increasing versatility and vehicle utilization.

Some of the pioneering COFDM applications include news cars or sports utility vehicles (SUV). In a typical configuration, a 2 m pop-up mast with a directional 30 cm antenna is combined with a roof-level omnidirectional antenna. The digital RF transmitter is placed on the roof adjacent to the antennas and can be automatically switched from directional to omnidirectional antennas as desired. (For example, using the pop-up mast and directional antenna for stationary shots requiring more system gain, and the omnidirectional antenna for mobile shots.) Inside the vehicle is a small rack housing the digital compression encoder and COFDM modulator.

For helicopter and fixed-wing applications, the RF transmitter is mounted on the lower side of the aircraft near the antenna pod, while the digital compression encoder and COFDM modulator are fitted inside the aircraft.

Digital vs analogue

You need to appreciate the fundamental difference between analogue and digital transmissions to see the advantages and disadvantages of each type of system.

The essential difference between an analogue signal and a digital signal is that the analogue signal amplitude can be any value between pre-defined limits. Analogue transmissions require significantly greater power and bandwidth than compressed digital transmissions, but the quality of the signal recovered can be very high.

In terms of microwave transmissions, this greater power can only be delivered by a larger transmit amplifier and/or a larger antenna than is required for a digital transmission.

Digital transmissions are always compressed for SNG and DENG, so as to acheive savings in power and bandwidth. The effect of the compression is that although at first glance the quality of the signal can look very good, there are particular picture degradations (termed artefacts) that can be objectionable on certain types of picture content – particularly fast-moving material and pictures with large areas of gradual colour change in the background.

However, as the cost of satellite capacity and the size of the SNG equipment are often primary considerations, these artefacts have to be tolerated as the compromise for the financial savings.

The compression process also increases the overall delay of the signal, as the processing involved in compressing and decompressing the signal takes an appreciable time. This is in addition to the delay that the signal suffers in travelling up from the earth to the satellite and back down to the earth, as we shall see later. Any delay can be problematical in conducting 'live' interviews.

Analogue is a wave signal
Digital is a binary 'on' and 'off' signal

Transmission and reception chains

In an analogue microwave link, the baseband video and audio signal from the camera and the microphone is connected to the input of the modulator. This takes the basic message signal and modulates it, using the FM process, turning it into an RF signal called the intermediate frequency (IF) signal typically based on a 70 MHz carrier. The output of the modulator is fed to an upconverter, which shifts the frequency of the IF signal from the relatively low 70 MHz frequency up to the super high frequency (SHF) of the microwave transmitter – typically in the 2.5, 5 or 7 GHz frequency bands. This is then amplified, fed to the antenna and transmitted as a microwave signal. The power of the transmit amplifier is typically between 5 and 15 Watt (W), where Watt is the measurement of power.

At this point we need to briefly mention decibels (dB). Often in signal processing we want to express ratios (particularly of power), and these can be clumsy to handle (remember working with fractions at school!). So engineers tend to talk in decibels. The convenience of using decibels is that multiplication and dividing of ratios can be performed by simply adding or subtracting values in dBs. The decibel is widely used in electronic engineering, and it is also a logarithmic unit – that is to say, 2 dB does not represent twice the power that 1 dB does (in fact, 3 dB is twice the power).

In our transmit amplifier, we have said it is typically between 5 and 15 W – and this corresponds to 7–11.75 dB in power. It is not necessary in this book to go into the maths, but you will see decibels cropping up from time to time.

The receiver consists of the mirror of this process. The received signal is picked up by the antenna, boosted by a low noise amplifier, downconverted from SHF to 70 MHz, and then demodulated to recover the original video and audio baseband signal. Each end of this process is called a transmission and reception chain respectively.

For a digital COFDM link, the video and audio is fed via an MPEG-2 digital compression encoder, which then feeds the modulator. At the receive end, the output of the demodulator is fed to an MPEG-2 decoder. Often these modulator/demodulator processes are included within the encoder/decoder units.

Audio channels

In an analogue microwave link the audio channels are not transmitted directly but are instead added as sub-carriers to the main carrier signal.

The audio signal from the microphone or VTR is fed into the microwave link modulator, which converts the incoming audio signal into an extra narrow FM carrier that is mixed with the main FM video carrier signal.

Each audio channel is thus added as a sub-carrier, and typically there are at least two audio sub-carriers on a terrestrial analogue link – because we need to either carry stereo, which is a two-channel system, or separate audio channels for the atmospheric natural sound (or effects) at the scene, and the voice commentary from the reporter (or track).

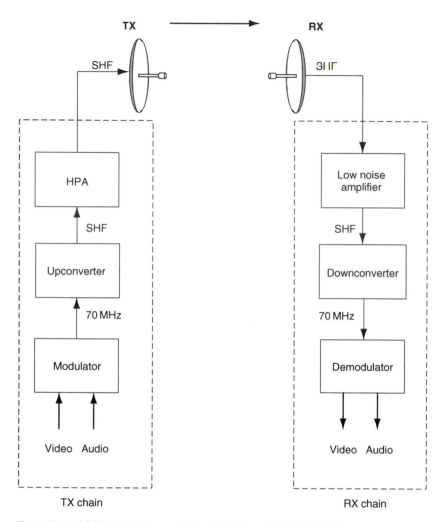

TX   →   RX

TX chain   **RX chain**

For a digital COFDM link, the modulator is fed via an MPEG-2 digital compression encoder, and the output of demodulator is fed to an MPEG-2 digital decoder. Often these modulator/demodulator processes are included within the encoder/decoder units.

Basic TX and RX chains

Why would we need to send the track and effects separately? Why not just send a single mix of the effects and the track together? Well, this helps in editing later, as having separate audio tracks allows the video editor the greatest flexibility when cutting different versions of the same story as it changes. It also allows different commentary track.

Handling of baseband audio – digital vs analogue

Audio is typically acquired and handled in analogue form, but it is possible that you may come across audio that has been converted into digital audio. We saw earlier how an analogue signal is converted to a digital one, and digital audio is commonly found in the broadcast studio environment.

The advantage of digital audio is that it is not affected by the transmission process (unless the transmission performance falls below a critical minimum level), and it can be embedded into a digital video stream and hence cannot get separated or misrouted. The disadvantage is that any manipulation of the audio – level, equalization (bass/treble boost/cut), etc. – is more difficult to carry out in the digital domain.

Hence it would be typical in ENG to make any changes to the audio while it is still in the analogue domain, and only digitize it (if required) at the point just before transmission. In general however, audio is handled as analogue in a ENG microwave link, except when digital microwave links are being used. Even then, as we have just noted, it is usual to carry out any production process while still as an analogue signal.

The audio that is fed to the link transmission chain is often fed via an audio mixer, as this gives the operator the opportunity of both making sure that the overall level is adequate, and also enable the mixing of sound from two sources – for example, a live 'talk-in' from the reporter with a live microphone to a piece of video pre-recorded and being played from the VTR in the truck. In an ENG truck, the audio mixer is often a small unit with 6–8 input channels, as opposed to the massive 32 or 48 input channel audio mixing desks found in large OB production trucks.

This is in essence the whole process. Obviously there is a good deal of sophisticated signal processing going on here, but so long as you understand this basic concept, you will be able to understand the setting up and use of microwave links.

Transmission and reception chains

Antennas

An antenna is another name for an aerial. It is essentially a device for radiating or receiving electromagnetic waves, and is vital in radio communication systems. There is little fundamental difference between transmitting antennas and receiving antennas, since the same antenna is often used for both purposes (as we shall see later when we look at SNG). While some antennas can be as simple as a wire thrown out of a window, for the best performance the right type of antenna needs to be used!

The most important properties of an antenna are its radiation pattern and its gain (magnification of the signal), whether it is being used at the transmitter or receiver. In the case of a transmitting antenna, the radiation pattern is a plot of the power strength radiated by the antenna in different directions. As a consequence of its radiation pattern, power radiated by an antenna may be concentrated in a particular direction, and this directivity is expressed in terms of power gain.

For a receiving antenna, the power received is defined by its collecting area – defined by the effective area of the antenna – and this is called its effective aperture.

Polarization

Before we discuss the different types of antennas, we should have a quick look at the subject of polarization, as it is relevant to antennas used in both terrestrial and satellite microwave communications.

Signals transmitted in any frequency band have a property termed polarization, and this relates to the geometric plane in which the electromagnetic waves are transmitted or received. Hence polarization describes the orientation of the electric field radiated from the antenna.

There are two types of polarization, circular and linear, and the reasons for choosing one over the other are many and varied. The property of polarization is related to the design of the antenna, and different polarizations may be used to allow the use of the same frequency; to minimize interference with an adjacent signal in frequency; or because a particular polarization may offer better propagation properties for the application.

Circular and linear polarizations are each further subdivided, and determine how the signal is transmitted from the feedhorn. Linear polarization is subdivided into vertical and horizontal polarizations. A horizontally polarized antenna radiates a horizontally polarized electromagnetic wave, a vertically polarized antenna radiates a vertically polarized electromagnetic wave, and a circularly polarized antenna transmits the electromagnetic wave rotating in a circular pattern. Circular polarization can be either clockwise (left-hand circular polarization – LHCP) or counter-clockwise (right-hand circular polarization – RHCP).

Generally speaking, an antenna set to one particular polarization will not detect or be interfered by signals of the opposite polarization, even though they may be at an identical frequency.

Microwave antennas come in a number of different shapes and sizes. Typically ENG microwave links utilize either parabolic (dish) or helix (rod) antennas, although occasionally omnidirectional antennas are used for a few specialized applications.

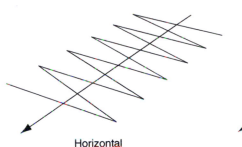

Horizontal

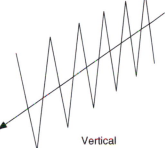

Vertical

Linear polarization

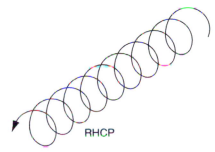

RHCP

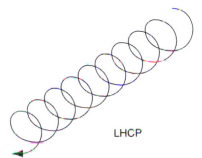

LHCP

Circular polarization

Parabolic antennas

In the majority of microwave systems, high gain antennas with very narrow beamwidth are required and this is achieved with parabolic or dish antennas of a reasonable size. A dish antenna has the optimum form for collecting electromagnetic radiation and bringing it to a focus. It acts rather as the reflector on a flashlight does – it concentrates and focuses the energy into a beam that is much stronger than the beam from the lamp itself. The parabolic antenna is essentially an electromagnetic lens, which just as a magnifying glass focusses sunlight energy into a narrow beam, focuses the RF electromagnetic energy into a narrow beam.

The reflecting surface of the antenna is based on a three-dimensional shape called a paraboloid, and has the unique property of directing all incoming wanted waves to a single point of focus. Reflective antennas are generally made of steel, aluminium, fibreglass or carbon fibre – the latter two with an embedded reflective foil.

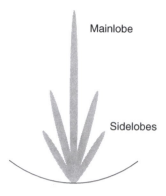

Mainlobe

Sidelobes

Main and side lobes

The parabolic reflector is very effective in rejecting unwanted signals and electrical noise – or unwanted electrical interference. Waves that enter at angles other than parallel to the main axis are reflected so as to miss the focal point altogether. There is a head unit or feedhorn placed at the focal point of the antenna. It is said to 'illuminate' the dish – this term is used even if the antenna is designed to only receive since reception is basically the reverse process of transmission, so the theory is common to both.

The antenna does not produce a completely perfect radiation pattern, which would be a single focussed beam, but has a main lobe (centred on the bore-sight) and a number of side lobes radiating out from the antenna.

One of the aims of good antenna design is to seek to minimize the side lobes while maximizing the main lobe – typically up to 70% efficiency – as too much energy in the side lobes will reduce energy in the main lobe signal.

The parabolic dish antenna is both highly directional and has a high gain (amplification). The maximum power possible from a link is defined by the addition of the dish gain and the amplifier gain. A clear line of sight is required for a long path length.

But in a city, perversely, high gain can be a disadvantage. In a cluttered city environment, the gain of the signal may be so great that multiple reflections of the signal are bounced off by other objects such as buildings near the path of the signal. This gives rise to the ghosting effect we spoke of earlier. The highly directional nature of the dish antenna can also mean that there can only be one path that will generally work. So a lower gain type of antenna may be used, as we shall shortly see.

Although we generally think of these antennas being circular in shape, they are not necessarily so. Nurad, a well-known American manufacturer, manufac-tures squared off parabolic antennas for use on ENG trucks.

The antennas vary in size from around 60 cm (2 feet) to 120 cm (4 feet) in diameter, depending on the application. The larger the antenna, the more focussed the beam, and the higher the gain.

Helix (rod) antennas

The helix or rod antenna (sometimes referred to as a 'golden rod', as it was originally a manufacturer's trade name for this type of antenna) is what is termed an end-fire antenna, and has circular polarization.

This antenna has a wire wound internally in the shape of a helix and the direction of winding on helical antennas is also important as it determines whether the wave will be left- or right-hand circularly polarized. The receiver must also be matched to the same design because it can only receive electromagnetic waves of a matching polarity. Maximum intensity of signal is along the axis of the helix, i.e. the axis of the rod. Typically the rod antenna is used in a dual configuration to give increased gain.

The rod antenna is less directional, but it is more advantageous in a city environment where the numbers of different paths that occur with a less-directional antenna are, perversely, an advantage. A number of paths can be generated, and with any luck at least one will find its way to the receiving antenna.

Ah, but what about multipath and ghosting? Surely that will degrade the signal. Yes it will, but if the paths are of a significantly different length, then the difference is so great in terms of the moment in time when the reflected signals arrive at the receiving antenna, that there is no significant degradation to the signal, and you can end up with usable pictures.

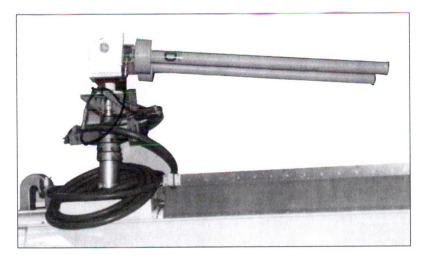

Helix (rod or end-fire) antenna (dual configuration) on a truck roof

Remember that we said it had circular polarization? Well, when a circularly polarized signal bounces off an object, the direction of polarization is reversed. This means at the receiver, the reflected signals arrive in opposite polarization and are therefore out of phase and not detected. But sometimes the best signal that is received is a 'bounce signal', in which case that is the signal the receiving antenna needs to pick-up, and so it needs to be set to the polarization opposite to that of the transmitting antenna!

Omnidirectional antennas

This type of antenna radiates a signal – as the name suggest – in all directions! Omnidirectional antennas at microwave frequencies for ENG/OB use can be relatively compact – they look like a short thick pole typically about 30 cm long mounted vertically. The disadvantage of this type of antenna is that the amount of gain in any direction is relatively low, and so the distance the link can travel and be received in good quality is reduced. However, there are certain applications where it has some advantages, as we will see later.

Flat plate antennas

There is another type of antenna that is sometimes used – the flat plate antenna. This antenna is essentially a small flat panel, 30–45 cm square for 2 GHz use, which is made of groups of tiny antennas which act together in phase to amplify the signal in the direction the plate is pointed. Different polarizations are available, but this type of antenna is only occasionally seen in ENG applications.

Trucks and masts

The thing about news is it can happen anywhere, and ENG equipment has to be both portable and reliable. This therefore means that the microwave link has to be portable (and reliable!), as it is deployed from base to a temporary location, rigged, used, and then de-rigged and taken either back to base or on to another story – all within a matter of hours.

There are different ways of using terrestrial microwave to cover a story. It can be mounted:

- on a truck, van or sports utility vehicle (SUV)
- in a helicopter or light aircraft to give live aerial shots
- carried on someone's back – a man-pack link
- mounted on the ENG camera itself.

We will start off by looking at vehicles, as this is by far the most common way of using ENG microwave.

When the microwave link equipment is fitted into a truck, it is also common for there to be space for some production facilities. This is because, as we have seen earlier, there is usually a need to both record and playback the material from a VTR, as well as offer some limited vision, switching and audio-mixing facility. Radio talkback is also often required, as we mentioned earlier, so the vehicle has to be large enough to be able to accommodate all of this equipment.

This is particularly true when you realize that the links truck will also have a telescopic mast, with the microwave transmitter unit and the antenna permanently mounted at the top. It is almost given that you will need height to achieve a clear get-away for the link, and the mast will (hopefully) help lift the transmitter clear of any local obstructions, and try to achieve a line of sight to the receiver. This means that the ENG vehicle will either be based on a large panel van, an SUV, or a four-wheel drive vehicle.

Trucks and masts

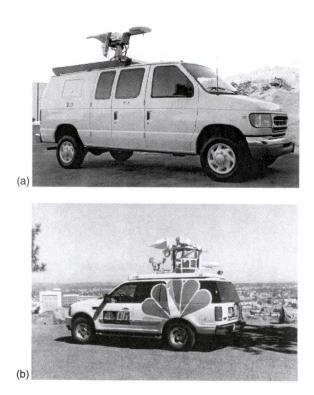

(a)

(b)

Types of ENG trucks (a © Wolf Coach; b © Frontline Communications)

The mast will typically extend to 12–17 m (40–55 feet), and is constructed as a series of hollow telescopic tube sections each extended by pumping compressed air into the mast base, pushing each of the sections up. This is called a pneumatic mast, as shown in the following figure.

Instead of using compressed air, some masts work by the use of tensioned cables within the mast, which are driven by a winch at the bottom – but pneumatic masts are the most common type found in use.

In addition to a control panel for the operation of the mast itself, the microwave transmitter at the top of the mast is operated from a control panel within the vehicle, which allows a number of settings (parameters) to be set and controlled. We will look at the operation of such a link in a moment.

The back of any ENG van (or SNG truck, for that matter) is used as an area for carrying all the ancillary items required to make live TV happen on any street corner.

The back of the vehicle typically carries the following:

- video and audio cables to connect a camera to the truck
- rubber matting to cover cables where they cross pavements, etc.
- rope and safety tape

Pneumatic mast on ENG vehicle

- mains cabling
- tools
- ladder for accessing the vehicle roof or other areas
- the kitchen sink!

The last point is actually quite serious. Particularly where a van is used by a number of different operators, there is a great temptation to add extra items 'just in case' without checking to see if they are already on board. The result can be an overloaded vehicle, as weight is a key issue in the operation of these vehicles. ENG and SNG vehicles are often built ending up fairly close to their maximum legally permissible weight, and there is often not enough consideration of all the extra equipment that gets added after it has left the manufacturer.

The back of a working ENG van

Setting up a link

Let us look in more detail at how the microwave link is set up for our live news transmission covering our story of the police shooting.

The ENG truck arrives on site at the hospital, as we said earlier, and the operator has to pick a spot which will enable a 'live' to be undertaken successfully (so it has to be within easy cabling distance of where the reporter is going to stand) but most importantly where the raising of the mast is going to be safe. Therefore, a spot has to be picked which is clear of any potential risks from overhead hazards – electricity supply cables, telephone lines, tree branches, etc.

Most links vehicles have stabilizers – either one or two pairs of retractable legs – which are designed and fitted so that the inevitable rock in the vehicle suspension is minimized. This is important as the effect of people climbing in and out of the van can make the mast rock, causing the microwave beam to go off target alignment.

The stabilizers are either fitted as a pair at the rear of the vehicle, at the middle of the vehicle, or there may be two pairs at the front and rear. The number and position is dependant on the size and length of the vehicle, in combination with the maximum extended height of the telescopic mast.

Having picked the spot, the 'links operator' deploys the stabilizers (if fitted) and then raises the mast. It is absolutely crucial that the operator clearly watches the mast as it rises, as a cable snagging or an unseen overhead obstruction can suddenly cause a serious accident.

The equipment at the top of the mast is connected to the equipment below by means of either cables, which are bunched together and 'loomed' to the mast at each mast section junction, or they are enclosed in an expanding plastic sheathed coil which extends as the mast rises. The sheathed plastic coil is typically known as a 'Nycoil', which is a brand of brightly coloured air-brake hose which you often see connecting a trailer to a commercial tractor unit. This type of polyurethane hose is highly suitable for carrying cables up a retractable mast, as it automatically collapses in a 'kink-proof' fashion.

The mast is now fully extended, and we are ready to align the link. The operator calls the studio or master control room (MCR) back at the station, either by a dedicated radio channel if the station has its own radio channels, or using a cellphone. (Refer to page 59.)

As we saw earlier, the frequency band used for microwave links is divided up into channels (just like the channels on your TV set) and the channel that is going to be used will probably have been assigned for this particular story – so let us say the operator is told by the station that he is to use channel 5, and that happens to be at a frequency of 2.58 GHz with horizontal transmit polarization.

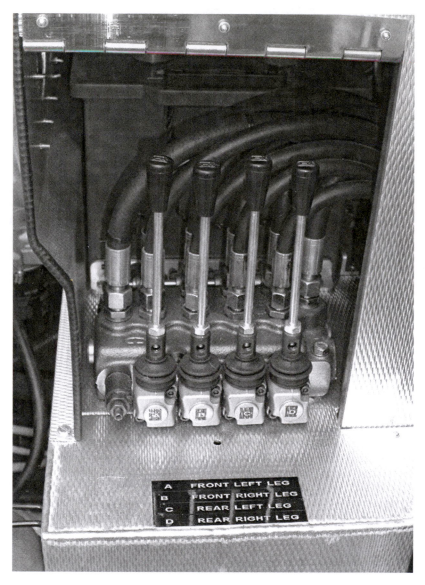

Stabilizer controls

The operator then needs to align the ENG truck antenna so that it is pointing approximately in the direction of the microwave receiver. The operator can do this by remotely controlling the pan and tilt head at the top of the mast. (Refer to pages 59 and 60.)

Nycoil (the red tubing) on a mast with an antenna

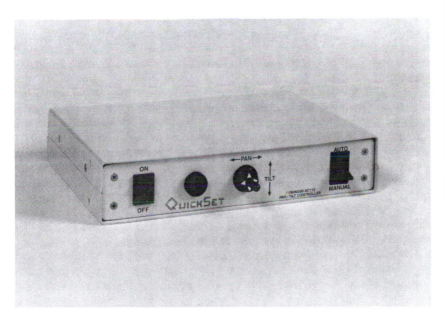

Quickset control panel (© Quickset Inc.)

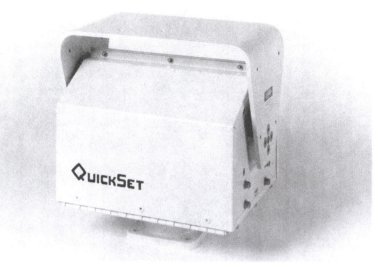

Quickset pan and tilt head (© Quickset Inc.) – without the transmitter and antenna

The receiver antenna may either be at the TV station itself or perhaps on a nearby high point – a building, hill or even a mountain! In this case there will be permanent circuits that connect the receiver to the station that carry not only the received video and audio signals, but also allows the station to remotely control the receiver equipment and antenna at the reception site, as shown opposite.

The operator will first switch his microwave transmitter into transmit on channel 5, with a test signal applied – typically colour bars on the video, and a 1 kHz steady tone on the audio channels. The operator will usually have some kind of 'ident' on the colour bars – the number of the truck and/or its location – and then check with the MCR at the station whether they can see his signal. It is very unlikely that they will initially, so the operator is talked in by the operator in the MCR at the station to achieve optimum alignment of the link. This is done as follows.

The operator makes a horizontal sweep of the arc of about 30° on either side of the direction of the microwave receiver (we describe this as the azimuth). If everything is alright, the MCR engineer, who is watching the output from the microwave receiver (set to channel 5 frequency and the antenna selected to the correct polarization) will call out to the truck operator (either via mobile cellphone or a radio) as soon as a flicker of the transmitted signal is seen. The truck operator will then make fine adjustments to azimuth from side to side to ensure that the receiver is 'seeing' the main signal lobe.

Central London receive point on a rooftop

The transmit antenna will actually radiate a main lobe (the maximum signal strength) and a number of weaker side lobes. In the MCR it is possible to be fooled that you have actually found the main lobe when in fact you may have optimized on a side lobe – which could lead to problems later if the weather worsened, or some other anomaly occurred.

The truck operator should sweep the antenna so that the MCR operator can see both the main lobes and the weaker side lobes – the main lobe can then be clearly identified as the one that generally gives the strongest signal.

The MCR engineer will not only rely on visual cues to identify the main and side lobes – the receiver produces a reading called the automatic gain control (AGC). It is not necessary to understand exactly what the AGC is – in short, it produces a reading on a meter or display that is a measurement of the received signal strength. The MCR engineer will know when the truck operator has pointed the antenna in the optimum direction by a mixture of the received video and audio signals seen and heard, along with the AGC reading.

Having aligned on the main lobe in the horizontal (azimuth) axis, the truck operator – with the MCR engineer still watching – will adjust the alignment of the antenna in the vertical (elevation) plane. This should again be a peak when the transmit antenna is exactly on axis with the receive antenna.

The MCR engineer may suggest that the truck operator tries a 'tweak' in elevation if it proves difficult to find a peak in the initial azimuth sweep. Unless the link is very strong and easily established, the whole process of aligning the link is an iterative process, so that the very best received signal can be obtained.

Some stations have steerable receive antenna rather than a fixed one, so the MCR engineer may steer the receive antenna to also optimize the receive end of the link once the truck operator has made all the azimuth and elevation adjustments at his end.

What is important is that the process is carried out in a methodical manner – if both ends of the link are steered at the same time, the process becomes chaotic and confused. Each 'end' must be clear about both what they are doing and what the other 'end' is doing.

So what are the common errors made in aligning the link? Some of these may seem obvious and stupid, but anyone experienced in setting up microwave links will recognize these errors because they will all have made them at one or another!

- Not having the correct azimuth bearing for the transmitter and the receiver (i.e. pointing the wrong way!)
- The transmitter and the receiver not being on the same channel (frequency)
- The transmitter or the receiver being set to the wrong polarization
- The transmitter or the receiver not being switched on (it happens!)

With the link correctly aligned and optimized for the best reception of the signal, the MCR engineer checks that the video and audio levels are correct, and that the communications with the truck are working.

The MCR engineer then routes the video and audio from the remote microwave to the studio.

The truck operator will then check that all the connections have been made via the cable termination panel (CTP) on the vehicle, which allows for the video, audio and talkback/IFB connections to and from the live camera position, as shown opposite.

The studio will then talk directly to the operator in the truck, and check communication with the reporter (often referred to as the 'talent'). As we have seen, communication with the reporter is all important, as for the typical 'live' shot there is likely to be a fair few questions and answers bouncing back and forth between the studio and the remote location – the hospital in our case.

From this point on, the work involved in maintaining the microwave link is limited to the MCR engineer keeping an eye on the incoming signal. The operator in the truck will be focussed on ensuring that the comms are working and the reporter is ready to go 'live'. The studio will then come to the reporter, who will do the 'live' insert.

After the 'live' shot, the reporter and/or the operator will check whether anything more is required from that location, and if not, pack up and move on to the next location or back to base.

Cable termination panel on a truck

Mid-points

Although less used nowadays in the age of SNG, we should just mention the option of mid-points, as these are used by stations who still use terrestrial microwave for long-haul links and have not yet been able to afford to enter the expensive world of SNG.

Microwave links over very long distances can be achieved by using a succession of point-to-point links – a chain of microwave repeaters termed 'mid-points' – that receive and then retransmit the signal on to the next point in the chain.

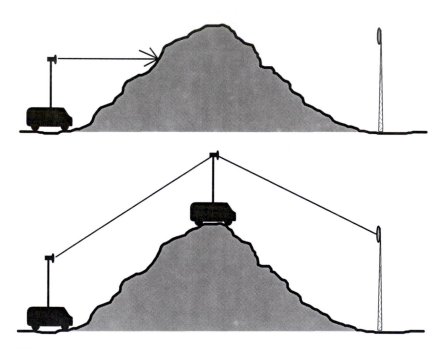

Mid-point

The mid-point is typically either a truck fitted with both a receiver and a transmitter with suitable antennas parked on a hill, a receiver/transmitter link on top of a mobile hydraulic hoist platform (cherrypicker); or a portable micro-wave receiver/transmitter link mounted on a tripod on a city centre rooftop.

Rigging microwave link on a 'cherrypicker' (60 m extension)

A microwave link can be mounted on a tripod for a temporary transmission, though it often needs to be secured to prevent it being blown away in bad weather. A tripod mounted link can also be used on the roof of a four-wheel drive car if it has a strengthened roof platform.

Tripod mounted link

The setting up of a set of mid-points is relatively straightforward, and it is common to try to use alternating frequencies and/or polarizations to minimize any risk of reflections finding their way back into the previous link hop. Before the advent of SNG, this was a common way of creating a long-haul connection back to the station, but it suffers from the disadvantages of demanding a lot of resources in terms of time, equipment and manpower. However, it does provide a means of covering that all important story that is 100 km away over two ranges of hills using terrestrial microwave.

Roofs

When a microwave links truck even with a mast cannot get a signal out of a city centre, a microwave link can be set up on a roof, either on a tripod or mounted on a pole. This link might be referred to as a 'starter' link. The link is rigged on a roof – or a suitable balcony – and the 'live' camera is cabled to it. The link equipment can hopefully be transported up within the building – via a lift or stairs – but it sometimes requires lifting equipment by rope from the outside of a building.

The setting up of a link for a roof starter link is just the same as for a mid-point – except obviously there is no receiver to be set up. The rigging of links on the roofs of buildings and other high points can be fraught with difficulties (such as finding cable routes, access and the risks of bad weather), and the issue of safety in these conditions is of paramount importance – we will look at this later.

Other microwave link platforms

The use of helicopters and light aircraft for ENG/OB microwave is often seen on sporting events, when either the event is spread out over a large area (such as the Tour De France cycle race, or city marathons), or if the sense of the event is enhanced by an aerial view – such as a major soccer or baseball tournament.

Airship links

Indeed, for stadium team sports it is common to use an airship or 'blimp' as this has the advantage of being able to hover indefinitely over a single position, or be able to move at a sedate pace to keep up with the event. It also has the advantage of being a lot cheaper to keep in the air than a helicopter, but has the disadvantage of being far more susceptible to bad weather (particularly high winds).

Helicopter links

Helicopters have a number of advantages – they can be quick to deploy, are able to get good camera views of an event (as their use by many police forces is testament to), and can provide a very viable aerial platform for microwave links. There are a number of microwave systems that are specially adapted to aerial use, and typically include an auto-tracking antenna, which will always point towards the receiver whatever the movement of the helicopter. The range of the link can be extended to over 200 km with suitable transmitter power, and helicopters are commonly used in the United States on local stations to give live traffic reports – a major drive to attracting viewers.

'Live' traffic report helicopter (© Wescam Inc.)

It is worth noting that helicopters are a hostile environment for electronics, principally due to the vibration picked up through the air frame. This is particularly an issue in the digital domain, where the degree of stability required to pass a digital signal through a compression and COFDM transmission system is very challenging. Slight variations in frequency can destroy the COFDM transmission.

However, in other respects, helicopters are the ideal platform for the use of COFDM links. Traditional FM analogue microwave transmissions from helicopters suffer from fading, break up, audio and video interference, and ghosting. Any microwave transmission from a moving source can be particularly susceptible to dynamic interference, characterized by signal 'dropouts', moving multiple ghosting, and severe colour and audio noise fluctuations. Transmission from a helicopter in flight will certainly generate a significant number of reflections.

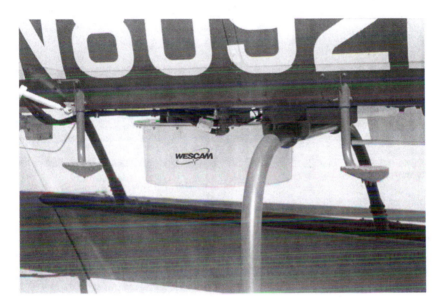

Microwave radome (cover) (© Wescam Inc.)

Because COFDM is especially resilient in an environment rich in bounced signals, it is a transmission system that has been seen to suit use on helicopters – as a standard COFDM was actually developed in part to suit mobile applications on vehicles.

A helicopter can also be used as an aerial mid-point, where the signal has to perhaps be carried over a range of mountains. It is a lot easier to put the mid-point in the helicopter than have to scale a mountain to rig the equipment! The issue of course is cost – helicopters are expensive machines, and their use in this respect is diminishing (as with mid-points in general) as the use of satellites can achieve the same result at a lower cost. Helicopters are also susceptible to weather conditions, whereas in general an SNG uplink is not.

Other microwave link platforms

Helicopter equipped with link and gyro-stabilized live camera (ball at front houses the camera) (© Wescam Inc.)

Man-pack links

On occasions, a microwave link needs to be more portable than simply being mounted on a truck – sometimes it needs to be carried by a person. Such links are called 'man-pack' links, and are much smaller and lighter units than those mounted on tripods or on truck masts. Typically, the link transmitter is a little larger than a pack of cigarettes, powered from a camera battery, feeding either a small horn type of antenna (which needs to be pointed in the direction of the receiver) or uses an omnidirectional antenna. The equipment is usually mounted onto a back-pack, with the antenna projecting above the head of the operator.

Man-pack type microwave links are typically used for short-haul operation in stadiums or in crowd situations where the camera needs to rove without the encumbrance of a cable connection. However, they are being superseded by camera mounted links, usually referred to as radio cameras or 'radio-cams'.

Man-pack link

Radio cameras

There are occasions when it is not feasible to physically connect the camera to the microwave or SNG truck, and therefore another means has to be used. Cable-free cameras or radio cameras provide complete freedom of movement for the camera operator to obtain interesting shots or to follow fast action.

Examples when this might occur are:

- where the cameraman is going to be moving around a good deal to different shooting positions
- where the physical distance between the camera and the truck is further than is feasible to connect with a cable
- when running a cable means crossing an area that has a lot of people (particularly crowds) walking across it
- where the camera is going to be used on a moving vehicle, such as at a horse race where the camera is going to run alongside the track keeping pace with the runners and riders.

The solution to this scenario is to use a compact low-power short-range microwave link between the camera and the truck, which carries both the video signal and the accompanying audio. This type of camera set-up is commonly called a 'radio-cam'. The link mounts on the rear of the camera, and is powered from the camera battery. Radio-cams have been used for years in sports, news and OBs. Unfortunately, with analogue transmission the pictures often break up, as the problem is that the signal bounces off walls, vehicles, trees and people, which distorts the received signal.

The biggest problem in using such a link is maintaining a clear path between the antenna on the back of the camera and the receiving antenna on the truck, and failure to achieve this leads to problems. Therefore the options are:

- separately mount the antenna on a pole, carried by an assistant, who keeps the antenna pointing towards the receive antenna
- use an omnidirectional antenna
- use an auto-tracking antenna.

The disadvantage of the first option is obvious – it requires another person, and the pointing of an antenna on the pole could very well be difficult in a crowded situation. It is viable if the cameraman is going to stay in one position, or within a fairly closely defined area.

The second option is commonly used on low cost radio-cam links, and for many situations is perfectly acceptable, though this needs careful co-ordination

Radio-cam

between the camera operator and the assistant. Commonly, problems are encountered when the signal is blocked or fading, causing picture and/or audio break-up.

The third option is the most flexible but also the most expensive. The auto-tracking system is actually a two-way system, where a control signal is transmitted back from the receiver to the camera-mounted antenna to steer the transmit antenna so that it can direct the camera-mounted antenna towards the receiver. Again, the signal fed back is derived from the AGC measured at the receiver. As an example of this type of system, we will look at the TRACS system developed in the United Kingdom.

Analogue radio-cam links
Analogue radio-cam links have been around since the 1980s, but they have always suffered from problems relating to path difficulties – fading, dropouts,

etc. Because of their poor reputation for reliability, they were never widely used, and when they were, they had to be set up days in advance and checked thoroughly – suitable for an OB, but not for a breaking news event.

In the 1990s, the BBC developed and licensed for manufacture a switched-antenna microwave camera link which provides a two-way video and audio link, which broadcast video and audio between the camera-mounted microwave unit (called C-TRACS) and a tracking microwave antenna system unit (called B-TRACS) at the truck. A return or reverse video feed can be sent from the base station to the camera viewfinder, as well as two-way talkback channel. The return video feed enables the cameraman to see what is actually being transmitted from the truck. The TRACS system was very effective, but due to its high cost is typically only used during major events such as premier soccer matches, where the cameraman is running up and down the touchline.

Digital radio-cam links

The problems with the simpler systems and the cost of the sophisticated systems like TRACS hindered the wider acceptance of radio-cams.

However, recently digital camera-mounted links using MPEG-2 digital compression have been developed, offering much better performance. Remembering that the signal transmitted by a COFDM needs to be digitally compressed, these systems offer exceptional signal robustness with minimal delay – and delay is the key here. We will look at this in more detail when we look at compression, but inevitably when a signal is digitally compressed, the signal is delayed as it goes through the encoding process. In addition, there is some delay in the COFDM process itself.

The significance of this in particular with a radio-cam is as follows. Imagine that a football match is being covered. A camera up in the stand area covers the winning goal. The director in the OB production truck then instantly cuts to the digital COFDM radio-cam on the touchline, and the picture from the digital radio-cam shows the ball going into the back of the net again – because the video is delayed due to the processing in compression and COFDM transmission. The original prototype of this type of camera had approximately 18 frames (3/4 s) of delay – which is a very large delay. The current production prototype has reduced this delay to 3 frames – which is just about acceptable. Hopefully this delay will be reduced to the optimum, which would be 2 frames or less.

Several manufacturers have developed compact digital links that fit onto the back of ENG camcorders, and some include bidirectional connectivity to give some remote control to the camera.

Camcorder mounted radio link (© Link Research)

Optical links

Infra-red optical video link

An alternative to using microwave signals is to use infrared light signals instead. In principle, this works like your TV remote control, but at very much higher power. An infrared link can be an effective alternative over distances up to 1000 m, and also offers freedom from any regulatory requirement, unlike microwave links used for broadcasting, no licence or permission is required for optical (infrared or laser) links.

The link has a transmitter and a receiver, as with a microwave link, and the units are both tripod mounted allowing transmission of video and audio up to 1 km with direct line of sight. Often, the transmitter and the receiver have built-in telescope sights and signal strength meters (AGC again) to assist in alignment.

The disadvantage of infrared links is their vulnerability to poor weather conditions such as heavy rain, mist or fog, as the wavelength of infrared light is affected by water droplets. The range of the link is optimum in clear weather, and so the distance of 1 km is the maximum that can be achieved – a more realistic working average is typically up to 500 m.

Optical laser link

Working at a much higher frequency, the optical laser link is a more expensive but reliable method of connecting two points without using microwave. As an example, we will look at a particular brand of laser link called Canobeam, made by Canon of Japan, which is widely used in newsgathering and event coverage.

Canobeam is an optical wireless communication system that enables a two-way wireless connection between two points by means of a powerful laser beam – and the distance between the locations can be up to 4.5 km due to the much greater power of the laser emitter. The Canobeam combines the optical accuracy of high quality lenses with the precision of a focussed laser.

Most importantly, unlike microwave signals, the use of Canobeam does not require any frequency allocation or license under telecommunications law in almost any country in the world. We will look at regulatory issues later in the book, but one of the biggest advantages of the optical laser link is that you can obtain as many channels as you need for the programme requirement without regulation. The Canobeam offers bidirectional transmission of four video channels (up to three in one direction) and ten audio channels – hence each end of the link is an integrated transmitter/receiver (termed a 'transceiver').

The Canobeam consists of two units – a base control unit and a head unit. The head unit is weatherproof (to a degree) and can be separated from the base unit by up to 50 m. The head unit is fully remote controlled and powered from the base unit.

The setting-up of any optical link – whether it be infrared or laser – is similar to setting-up a microwave link. Adjusting the optical sighting between two points can be very difficult because the laser beam is very narrow. However, the Canobeam has a small high power optical laser sighting system, and a monitoring camera built into the head unit. On the head unit, there is an optical viewfinder for pointing the units at each end so that they are approximately aligned in the correct direction. Each unit has a laser sighting 'flasher' which even in clear weather can be seen at up to the maximum operating distance of 4.5 km through the monitoring camera. The power of each transmission laser is then optimized for the distance between the transceiver units.

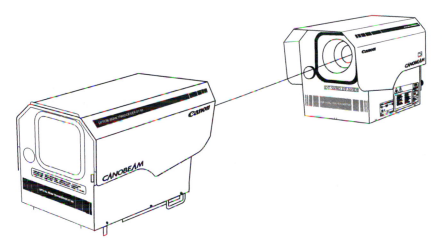

Canobeam link © Canon Japan

Fine adjustment of the direction of the beam is achieved by finely aligning the mirror in the head unit via a four-way touchpad on the base unit. As the beam reaches near the correct alignment axis, the mirror is locked into the optimum position by an auto-tracking system, which then maintains the optimum alignment by measuring the received signal from the other end.

The same process occurs at the other end of the link, and it generally takes less then 30 min to set up a Canobeam link. However, as with microwave (and unlike the infrared link), the Canobeam has to be used with care. While microwave, infrared and laser signals are all invisible to the eye, both microwave and laser are potentially hazardous. The Canobeam is classified as a Class 3B laser beam, which unlike the Class 1 laser in your CD player, is hazardous to the naked eye. However, the equipment has been manufactured such that the laser beam is diffused, and Canon states that the laser can be viewed directly for up to 7 min at a distance of 40 cm from the lens without risk of damage to the eye. Nevertheless, when using such equipment it should be treated with respect.

Optical links

Satellites and orbits

In October 1945, the famous science fiction author Arthur C. Clarke wrote an article which was published in a British radio hobbyist magazine. In that article, he put forward an idea about how the coverage of TV transmissions could be improved by using radio 'relays' situated above the Earth's atmosphere. These relays are what we now call communications satellites.

The principle of the satellite is that it can be put into an orbit at a distance of about 35 000 km from the Earth's surface so that as it orbits the Earth its speed of rotation exactly matches the speed of the Earth's rotation. The effect of this is that the satellite appears stationary from any point on the Earth's surface (geostationary) that can 'see' the satellite, and so antennas can be pointed in one direction and will always keep track of the satellite. If you have a satellite dish on your house for direct-to-home (DTH) satellite services, this is why it can be bolted down pointing in one direction, and it should never need to be moved again.

Geostationary orbit principles

The Earth completes one rotation on its North–South pole axis every 24 hours, and it can be calculated that at a specific distance from the Earth, a satellite in a circular orbit around the Earth will rotate at the same speed as the Earth. This will be essentially in an orbit where the centrifugal force of the satellite's orbit, throwing the satellite out into space, is equal to the Earth's gravity pulling the satellite towards the Earth.

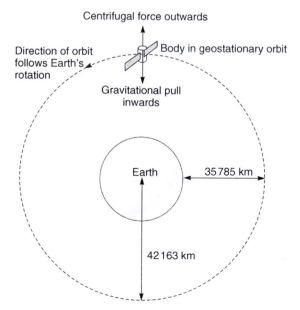

Geostationary orbit

If the satellite's orbit is directly above the Equator, then the satellite is said to be in a 'geostationary' orbit. The geostationary orbit is at a distance of 35 785 km above the Earth's surface at any point on the Equator, and satellites that are positioned in this circular orbit above the Equator are said to be in the 'geostationary arc'.

Currently, there are over 250 satellites in geostationary orbit, and in total over 8500 artificial satellites in various other types of orbits above the Earth, not only serving commercial telecommunications needs, but experimental, scientific observation, meteorological and military uses as well.

The position of a satellite within the geostationary arc is referred to by its longitudinal position relative to the Earth's surface.

So let us just briefly look at the subject of longitude and latitude, since the co-ordinates of longitude and latitude are used when pinpointing the position of a satellite transmitter or receiver on the Earth's surface. This is important for calculating the azimuth and elevation angles that are needed to correctly and accurately point the antenna at the satellite.

Longitude and latitude

Imagine that symmetrical lines run from the North to the South Poles – these are called lines of longitude (meridians), some of which are shown in the diagram overleaf. The line that runs through Greenwich in London, United Kingdom, is termed the Greenwich Meridian, and is the 0° longitude reference point. Lines run North to South around the complete 360° circumference of the Earth. Any point can be referred to as being at a certain point °E or °W of the Greenwich Meridian, depending on which direction around the Earth the point is being referenced. Satellite orbital positions in the geostationary arc are referred to in this way.

Similarly there are parallel lines that run in rings around the Earth from east to west between the North and the South Poles – these are lines of latitude or 'parallels'. The line that runs around the Earth at its middle is the Equator, and is the 0° latitude reference point. Lines of latitude run from 0° to 90° running from the Equator to the North (Northern hemisphere), and similarly 0° to 90° from the Equator to the South (Southern hemisphere). Any point is referred to as being at a certain point °N or °S, depending on whether it is in the Northern or Southern hemisphere respectively.

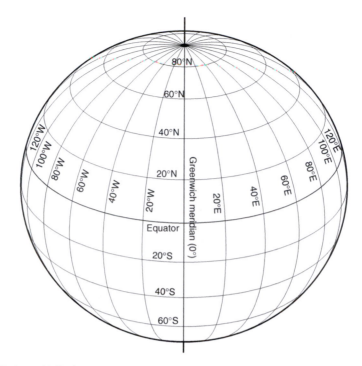

Longitude and latitude

Basic satellite communication theory

Uplinks – space segment – downlinks

A satellite receives a signal from a ground transmitter – the 'uplink' – and re-transmits ('reflects') the signal to a ground receiver – the 'downlink'. A satellite can be considered to have a number of these 'radio mirrors' – termed transponders. The part of the system in the sky is termed the 'space segment', as we saw on page 15. The signal takes a finite time to travel up to the satellite and back down to earth (referred to as satellite delay), and is around 250 ms.

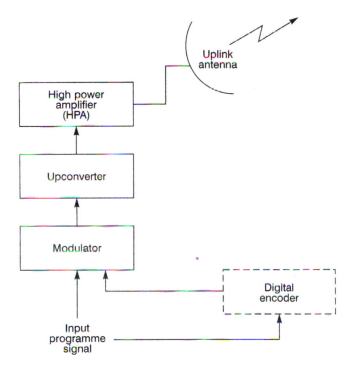

Uplink chain

As we look at the functions within a complete satellite transmission system, there are certain processes that are part of the uplink and the downlink which will be seen in principle to be common. The signal is modulated or demodulated, amplified, and converted up or down in frequency. The uplink is primarily composed of a modulator, an upconverter, and a high power amplifier (HPA), which is connected to an antenna (dish).

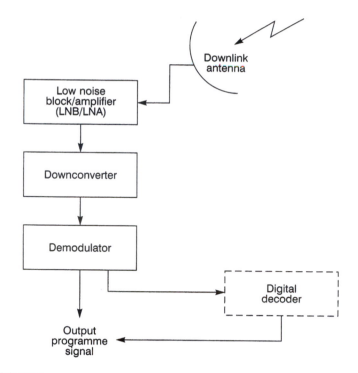

Downlink chain

Some form of monitoring of the uplinked signal would also be implemented. Additionally, for a digital system, there is an encoder – the digital compression component.

The downlink has an antenna, a downconverter, and a demodulator, and as with the uplink for the digitally compressed signal, a decoder, and typically there would also be a monitoring system able to measure parameters of the received signal.

Typically, the downlink antenna will be significantly larger than the SNG uplink antenna (from 4 to 30 m in diameter) and a location used for this is termed a 'teleport'. National telecommunication authorities, satellite operators, individual broadcasters and private enterprises operate teleports.

Basic digital SNG system

Before we look in detail at SNG systems, we need to clarify why in this book we are only going to consider digital and not analogue SNG systems.

Since around 1994, digital SNG uplinks have been made possible by the development of low bit-rate digital compression encoders. The development of digital compression encoders that could run at bit-rates as low as 8 Mbps created an opportunity for use for SNG, and this in turn led to the realization that more channels could be fitted on a satellite, which led to lower costs to use the satellite. So the advantage offered was lower power uplinks and narrower bandwidth channels on the satellite, offering the possibility of lower satellite charges. Instead of a 27 MHz channel for an analogue signal, a digital signal could be fitted into 9 MHz (nowadays often less), hence improving the efficiency of use by a factor of three.

The advances in the equipment for digital operation led in general to a reduction in size. Less power is required for digital operation, so antennas and amplifiers could be smaller, and so cost less. Later on, it was realized that by the use of digital 'multiplexing', several programme paths could be provided more cost-effectively than by the multiple RF chains which are required in the analogue domain.

Analogue systems were in common use in Europe until the mid-1990s, and in the United States to the present day. Satellite operators have encouraged the transition to digital in each market as it became ready, though there are a few markets where there is still usage of analogue SNG. Readers interested in this particular area should refer to the author's book 'Satellite Newsgathering', as this deals with both analogue and digital systems in much more detail.

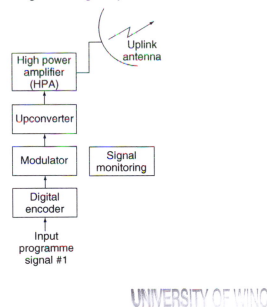

Basic DSNG system

Typical DSNG setup

Frequency bands of operation

There are two principal frequency bands used for satellite transmissions for TV, which include those used for SNG. The band in the frequency range of approximately 4–6 GHz is called the C-band, and the frequency band in the range of approximately 11–14 GHz is called the Ku-band, as shown in the figure opposite.

C-band

The C-band is the frequency band that has been used for telecommunication transmissions since the 1960s. The transmit frequency band is typically in the range of 5.8–6.5 GHz, and the receive frequency band is 3.4–4.8 GHz, and as far as SNG is concerned, C-band is used exclusively for digital transmissions.

C-band does have some limitations from a regulatory aspect, as its use for SNG transmissions is not permitted in Europe and many other areas of the world. The problem in developed countries is that this particular frequency band is widely used for terrestrial microwave links in fixed telecommunication networks.

On the other hand, the attraction of C-band for SNG transmissions is that in some other parts of the world there is no ad hoc satellite transponder capacity in the Ku-band available for SNG usage. Equally, in these same areas there is often no sophisticated telecommunication infrastructure to limit C-band SNG transmissions.

C-band can be used for analogue transmissions, but requires large uplink powers resulting in the requirement for large antennas and amplifiers. Hence

84

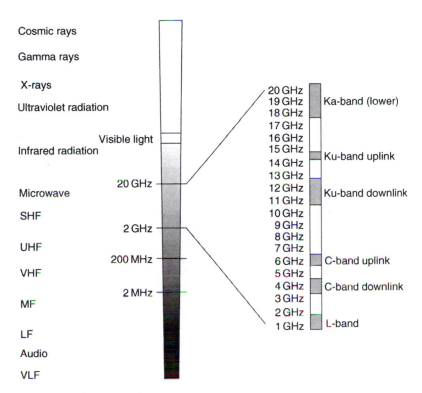

Cosmic rays	
Gamma rays	
X-rays	20 GHz
	19 GHz — Ka-band (lower)
Ultraviolet radiation	18 GHz
	17 GHz
Visible light	16 GHz
Infrared radiation	15 GHz — Ku-band uplink
	14 GHz
20 GHz	13 GHz
Microwave	12 GHz — Ku-band downlink
	11 GHz
SHF	10 GHz
2 GHz	9 GHz
	8 GHz
UHF	7 GHz
200 MHz	6 GHz — C-band uplink
VHF	5 GHz
	4 GHz — C-band downlink
2 MHz	3 GHz
MF	2 GHz
	1 GHz — L-band
LF	
Audio	
VLF	

Spectrum showing satellite bands

for SNG we use lower power digital transmissions in the C-band, with antennas and amplifiers similar in size to those used in Ku-band systems.

Ku-band

The Ku-band is the frequency band that is now, in many parts of the world, the predominant band for TV (particularly DTH services) and is the dominant frequency band for SNG.

The transmit frequency is typically in the range of 14.0–14.50 GHz, and the receive frequency is split into three bands, 10.95–11.7 GHz, 11.7–12.25 GHz and the upper band of 12.25–12.75 GHz.

It is used widely in areas that have a developed telecommunication infra-structure, such as Europe and the United States.

The antennas are small and the uplink powers required, are relatively modest. Hence very compact digital SNG systems can be easily transported between locations.

Basic digital SNG system

85

Dual band

Since 1995, a number of manufacturers have offered dual-band systems. They are termed dual band as the RF section of the system (which includes the HPA and the antenna) spans both the C- and Ku-bands.

The operational advantage is obvious for flyaways, as with a single system the user has the choice when travelling to a location of being able to operate in either frequency band, subject to satellite capacity being available and no regulatory restrictions.

The principal global newsgatherers find these systems particularly flexible, as it is not necessary to decide before departure which band the system is going to operate in, since the choice of frequency band can be left until arrival at the destination if available space segment cannot be determined at the time of deployment.

The additional components to enable the system to operate in both bands are relatively minor. It is simply a matter of making a front panel selection on the HPA to change bands. The only other component that is altered is the feed arm, and that generally fits onto the same antenna.

The only disadvantage of a dual-band system is the increased cost, as a separate feed arm for each frequency band has to be purchased, and a dual-band HPA is generally more expensive.

Polarization

The transmission of signals to and from satellites in either frequency band has the same property we saw earlier in terrestrial microwave – that of polarization.

Both circular and linear polarizations are used for satellite communications, and the signal is transmitted and received via the feedhorn – the assembly on the end of the arm extending out from the antenna.

This either delivers the signal into the focus of the transmit antenna on an uplink, or receives the signal via the focus of the receive antenna on a downlink.

The polarization on an SNG antenna can be adjusted by typically rotating the feedhorn, although some manufacturers provide adjustment by rotating the complete reflector and feed assembly.

As with terrestrial microwave links, the property of polarization is one of the defining parameters for a satellite transmission. Suffice to say that, in general, circular polarization is used in transmissions in C-band, and linear polarization is used in the Ku-band.

What is the reason for having different polarizations? Principally, the property of polarization allows the maximum utilization of frequency bandwidth on the satellite, as it enables the reuse of identical frequencies on the opposite polarization on the satellite.

Again, just to remind you from earlier, an antenna switched to one particular polarization will not detect or be interfered by signals on the opposite polarization, even when they are at an identical frequency.

However there is one important distinction from terrestrial microwave – which is a direct point-to-point system.

A satellite uplink transmitter has to transmit to the satellite downlink receiver via a satellite – it is an indirect point-to-point system. In general, in satellite transmissions, a signal transmitted (uplinked) from the ground on a particular polarization is received on the ground (downlinked) on the opposite polarization.

The uplink and the downlink antennas have operationally adjustable polarization (due to the effects of the position of the satellite and the effects of the Earth's curvature).

However, the significant element of a DSNG system is compression, so we need to look at this in more detail before we look at the whole uplink–downlink process.

Basic digital SNG system

Digital compression

Digital compression is now an essential characteristic of satellite transmissions, and as we have already seen, increasingly in terrestrial microwave as well. Compression is a highly complex subject, and to fully explain is far beyond the scope of this book, but we do need to have some concept of the process in order to understand its fundamental advantages (and disadvantages!).

So why would we want to compress a signal? The answer is that in an ideal world, we would not. If we had unlimited bandwidth available to us to send our information, then there would be no need for compression. Unfortunately, bandwidth is a valuable resource, and great efforts are made to make sure that there is efficient use of it.

Digital compression is essentially about squeezing large bandwidth signals into narrower available bandwidth (frequency spectrum). But satellite communication revolves around the issues of power and bandwidth, and by digitizing and compressing the signal, we can reduce demand for both power and bandwidth – and hence reduce cost.

Hence there is a need to strip out the redundant and insignificant information in the signal thus producing a compressed signal.

The process of compression can be likened to the use of concentrated orange juice.

Squeezing the juice

Consider a carton of concentrated orange juice that you buy in a supermarket. Before you picked it up off the shelf, the process began with squeezing oranges to produce orange juice, of which the major constituent is water.

The water is removed to produce a concentrate that can be put into a small carton and transported to the shop for sale. The customer buys the orange juice concentrate, takes it home, and reconstitutes the orange juice by adding back in water.

Effectively, the orange juice is compressed (just like the signal), so that a comparatively large volume can be transported in a small carton (or bandwidth), and then the juice is reconstituted by adding the equivalent volume of water back in that was removed in the first place (decompressed).

What is the advantage of this to the consumer? Because a relatively large amount of orange juice has been reduced to a smaller volume in the carton, the costs of transportation are much lower, the orange juice can be kept on the shelf for longer, and does not need as much care and attention in storage and transportation as fresh juice.

Because of these factors, the cost of the concentrated orange juice is much less than the freshly squeezed juice, and is therefore much more affordable.

But there is a compromise, as I hear you say 'Ah, but it does not taste the same as freshly squeezed juice' – and that inevitably is also the result of the compression processes we will be looking at.

Just as the reconstituted juice is not quite the same as when it began life after being squeezed from the fruit, at the end of the compression and decompression process the signal is never quite the same as the original – something is lost along the way, just as with the orange juice.

However, it costs less in the end, and is a reasonable facsimile of the original for most people. But there should never be any doubt that a signal that has been compressed, transported and decompressed (reconstituted) will never be the same as the original.

So, compression is necessary to reduce the amount of bandwidth used on the satellite, and hence reduce the cost of space segment. Increasingly the process of digital compression is far more efficient and cost-effective as it uses technology developed for computers.

Pixels

In digital video compression, each frame of the TV picture can be considered as being made up of a number of picture elements ('pixels'): a pixel is the smallest element that can be seen by the human eye and measured (quantified) in a picture.

Each pixel is measured – sampled – and this sample is then an instantaneous measurement of the picture at a particular point in time. As we learnt earlier in the description of the TV picture, a TV frame is made up of a number of lines (625 or 525), and a picture can be divided up horizontally and vertically into a number of pixels – and in a TV picture, pixels in the horizontal direction correspond with the lines of the TV picture.

The number of pixels defines the resolution or sharpness of the picture. This is the same as the way a photograph in a newspaper is made up of individual dots of ink – the more dots per millimetre, the greater the resolution or detail of the picture.

Principles of compression – digital sampling

We covered digitization of a signal earlier, but just to recap, a digital signal conveys information as a series of 'on' and 'off' states, which is represented as the numbers '1' and '0' in binary arithmetic.

In a stream of 1s and 0s, each 1 and each 0 is termed a bit, and a signal is transmitted at a certain speed or bit-rate, measured in bits per second (bps). The analogue signal is converted to a digital signal by a process called sampling. Sampling is when a signal is instantaneously measured, and the value of the signal at that instant is converted to a binary number. The signal is typically sampled thousands (for audio) to millions (video) of times per second.

The more accurate the binary number obtained from each sample, the better the quality of the signal that can be transmitted, and the more accurate the original signal can be reproduced. The greater the number of bits per sample, the more precise is the instantaneous value of the signal obtained. These bits are transmitted at a given data rate, expressed usually in million bits per second (Mbps) because of the huge number of bits to be transmitted.

In both DSNG and DENG, digital transmissions are typically compressed down to a rate of 8 million bits per second (8 Mbps) or lower. For higher quality, the bit-rate may be as high as 18 Mbps, but this is usually only for very high quality event or sports coverage.

The original standard for digital video was published as the European standard CCIR Rec. 601 standard. In general, digital video at broadcast quality is loosely referred to as '601' video, and an uncompressed digital video signal has a data rate of 270 Mbps. Signals at this data rate are referred to as serial digital interface (SDI) as the digits are transported as a 'serial' stream of data (as opposed to a parallel stream). The significance of this is that particularly in DSNG trucks, the baseband video is processed and transported between equipment within the truck as an SDI signal. Additionally, some ENG camcorders are capable of producing an SDI output on the rear of the camera, which can make subsequent handling of the signal much easier. Audio, on the other hand, is generally left in analogue form up until the input to the digital compression encoder.

An SDI signal is over thirty-three times the data rate of the typical 8 Mbps DSNG/DENG signal, and this data rate of 270 Mbps, when modulated would require over 250 MHz of bandwidth.

It is not feasible to allocate this amount of bandwidth on commercial satellite systems or terrestrial microwave bands, hence the need for compression.

Video is typically sampled at 10 bit accuracy (i.e. 10 bits are used to describe each sample), with a sample for each luminance pixel value and also for each of the two colour difference pixel values. Thus we have separate streams of samples for luminance and for each of the chrominance difference signals.

Redundancy

Once a signal has been digitized, the signal is a bit stream at a given overall data rate. Within that data stream, there will inevitably be sets of data that are repeated, and the repeated sections represent redundancy in the signal (like the water in the orange juice).

The aim of any compression system is to remove as much redundancy in the information signal as possible to minimize the bandwidth or data rate required.

Compression depends on flaws in human psychovisual and psychoacoustic characteristics – these describe human sensory perception in sight and hearing.

Digital compression is 'perceptive' compression, since the results are pictures and sounds that 'trick' the brain into thinking that the material looks and sounds like the original. Looking at our orange juice analogy, we know that the taste of the reconstituted juice is 'perceptively' close to the original – but not identical.

With the orange juice, we removed the redundant component – water – to achieve the compression. That is the essence of video and audio compression – to remove the redundancy in the signal.

So how do we identify which are the redundant parts of the signal? In any frame of a TV picture there are parts of the image that have the same values of brightness and colour in particular areas. So, instead of sending a repeating string of numbers that represent individual values of brightness and colour in these areas, one string of numbers can be sent that represent brightness and colour in these parts of the image that are essentially the same.

In audio, there are parts of the signal that can be removed without the brain noticing the difference. The standards used in digital newsgathering signal compression integrate both the audio and the video into a single combined (multiplexed) signal.

Digital compression

Video compression

The aim in video compression is to remove those parts of the signal which we do not essentially need.

The reason why video compression works so well is that video data is described as being 'very redundant', due to the way the human psychovisual system operates. There are three types of redundancy in video:

- spectral (brightness and colour)
- spatial (similarities in parts of the picture)
- temporal (similarities between one TV frame and the next).

Spectral redundancy

Bright pixels tend to be bright in all three colours, red, green and blue, and therefore there is said to be spectral redundancy – the similarity between colour values at any one point in the picture.

Earlier we mentioned the ability to fool the human brain into thinking that it is seeing a true representation of the original picture. This extends to how the brain is able to distinguish the brightness (luminance) and colour (chrominance) detail of a picture.

The human eye is much better at distinguishing brightness differences than colour differences. This can be used to an advantage in conveying colour information, as there is less precision required – a higher level of precision would be 'wasted' as the brain is unable to make use of the additional information and distinguish the difference.

When digitizing a video signal, fewer samples are required to convey the colour information, and fewer samples means less bandwidth. Typically, for every two luminance samples there is only one chrominance sample required.

Spatial redundancy

In the digital domain the removal of further redundant information is carried out in two dimensions within each frame of picture, described as spatial redundancy (i.e. relating to a frame of space).

Spatial redundancy is the relationship each pixel has with the neighbouring pixels around it – more often than not, two neighbouring pixels will have very nearly the same brightness and colour values.

Consider one frame of a picture signal. Suppose that within this frame there is a notable area of the picture that has either the same colour or brightness content – or both.

The luminance and/or chrominance would be the same across this similar area, and therefore instead of sending the same numbers for each and every sample, one number could be sent representing a block of sample points in an area where the information content remains the same.

Hence we have found some spatial redundancy, and this reduces the amount of data that has to be sent.

Temporal redundancy

In a TV picture, there is a sense of motion because there is a difference in the position of objects between one frame and the next.

Objects that have moved in the time between one frame and the next often may not significantly change shape, so by sending the same information from one frame to the next, some redundancy in the data from one frame to the next can be removed. This redundancy between successive frames is described as temporal redundancy (temporal meaning it relates to time).

Consider two frames of a picture signal. In the first frame, there is an object that is also present in the second frame – for example, let us presume that the first frame has a building in it.

Unless there is a shot change or a rapid camera pan, the building will be the same shape and present in the next frame (though not necessarily in the same position if the camera has moved slightly).

The block of data samples that described the building in the first frame could therefore be repeated in the second frame. In fact, most pictures shot in a single sequence are remarkably similar from one frame to the next, even in a moderately quickly moving sequence – only 1/25 (PAL) or 1/30 (NTSC) second has elapsed, which is much faster than the blink of an eye!

Therefore there is a significant scope for data reduction by simply reusing sets of data sent for the previous frame, albeit that the blocks of data may have to be mapped (moved) to a different position in the frame.

MPEG

MPEG stands for Motion Picture Experts Group, an organization established in 1988 to develop digital compression standards for video and audio material in the multimedia world.

Its work is not exclusively within the field of broadcasting – its remit is much wider than that – and it now works on standards that are used over the Internet.

The MPEG broadcast standard defines the way the audio and video are compressed.

MPEG-2

This is the standard used for a wide variety of applications, including DTH broadcasting by satellite and digital terrestrial TV delivered to the consumer.

It is a truly global standard used in a very wide variety of applications from computers to HDTV, with a range of bit-rates from 2 to 80 Mbps.

The MPEG-2 standard was published in 1995 primarily for digital TV broadcasting, and is the dominant compression standard for DNG.

Profiles and levels

MPEG-2 consists of many different types of service, classified under Profiles and Levels, which allow 'scaling' of the video.

The principal standard used for digital video broadcasting is described as main profile/main level. It is far beyond the scope of this book to describe exactly what that means, but broadly the Profile defines the data complexity and the chrominance resolution (sharpness), while the Level defines the overall image resolution and the maximum bit-rate per profile.

4:2:0 and 4:2:2

There are two ways of referring to digital video signals, based on the way they are sampled.

Digital video regarded as 'full-quality' is referred to as 4:2:2, while 4:2:0 refers to a digital video signal which has approximately half the number of chrominance samples of 4:2:2.

The 4:2:0 standard is the compression used in DTH services. In the early days of MPEG-2, 4:2:0 encoders were the norm for DSNG, as the encoders were simpler and therefore cheaper, but with the advances in MPEG-2 encoder technology, it is common nowadays to use 4:2:2 encoders as they are now almost as cheap as 4:2:0 encoders (4:2:2 encoders can also operate in 4:2:0 mode).

The coding is either defined as 4:2:0 MP@ML (Main Profile @ Main Level) or 4:2:2 MPEG-2. 4:2:0 and 4:2:2 describe the type of luminance and chrominance sampling and processing.

DVB and MPEG-2

We have the option of multiplexing (mixing) two programme paths (or 'streams') in the digital domain by cascading two digital compression encoders together to provide a single digital data stream to the uplink chain.

Each stream is not affected by the other, but they are cleverly mixed together to form a single stream of data. At the receiving end, each programme stream can be selected and separated.

This is defined by the DVB standard, which enabled the start of DTH services via satellite in many parts of the world.

In the DVB standard a key feature is programme security, so that for services delivered to the home, only those who have paid for a service may receive it. As a result the DVB standard allows for conditional access (CA) using a security key.

This method of applying a security key (scrambling) is used on some DSNG feeds where there is a fear that the material may be 'hijacked' by the unscrupulous, or where the material contained in the feed has a high degree of exclusivity.

MPEG-2 transmissions are either transmitted as single channel per carrier (SCPC), or multiple channel per carrier (MCPC) feeds – combining several programme channels together.

However, at an individual programme channel level, both techniques use the same method for building a data stream containing the video, audio and timing information. This combination of compressed video and audio is termed a transport stream (TS).

Since many of the MPEG-2 encoders used for DNG are derivatives of those used in programme distribution, the ability to multiplex streams together is either an integrated part of the encoder, or an external multiplexer can be used.

The streams are combined at the uplink, and the downlink de-multiplexes the TS back into separate streams by using the packet identifier (PID) value, which is the channel identifier containing all the navigation information required to identify and reconstruct a programme stream.

PID values are entered into the MPEG decoder to enable reception of the signal, and are the same values as those entered into the MPEG-2 encoder at the origination of the transmission.

MPEG

MPEG picture problems

Artefacts

When pushed to the limit, compression processes can produce visual defects, termed 'artefacts'.

These include a pixellation effect commonly referred to as 'blockiness', momentarily showing as rectangular areas of picture with distinct boundaries. Other artefacts may be seen near the edges of objects, such as blurring caused by reducing horizontal and/or vertical resolution. However, one of the most commonly seen problems is colour quantization error, often obvious on smooth areas of changing colour shade, where there are seen to be distinct bands marking the transition from one shade to another of a similar hue.

Delay and latency

Delay through a compression process is termed latency, and latency is of particular concern in DSNG and DENG operations.

The interaction in a 'live' two-way interview requires that both the questions and answers are delivered as smoothly as possible, but the delay of the compression process which is then added to the fixed satellite delay means that these interviews often have an awkward hesitancy about them.

This can be masked to a degree by imaginative techniques used both in the studio and out in the field, but there is always the evident hesitation between interviewer and interviewee. These compression delays ('latency') have reduced as the computational advances in processing speed have increased.

The viewer is also growing more tolerant of these delays to the point where they are hardly noticed, and so the problems are diminishing as time passes.

Some coders also offer a facility to improve the latency at the expense of movement compensation – the so-called interview or low delay mode. This is selected via the front-panel menu on the MPEG-2 coder, reducing the overall processing time of the signal.

Changing production techniques is by far the best way to try to overcome these awkward pauses. It is common for the studio to cue the reporter a fraction of a second earlier than normal, so that by the time they respond, the delay has passed unnoticed.

Often you will see reporters in the field looking thoughtful or slowly nodding after they have replied to a question, so that it makes their eventual answer to the next question look as if it is a very carefully considered reply! Like many other things in TV, much can be achieved by using 'smoke and mirrors'!

These techniques of course do not work if it is a straight 'down the line' interview with a member of the public, who naturally is unaware of these tricks of the trade.

However, you can often see this all going horribly wrong even with a seasoned reporter if there is a studio presenter asking questions who does not appreciate the subtle techniques required to cope with satellite and compression delay.

Classically this happens when part way through the answer from a reporter in the field, the presenter interjects with a supplementary question or comment. The field reporter carries on for a second or so, then halts in their tracks, meanwhile the studio presenter realizes their mistake and urges the reporter in the field to continue – and you get a cycle of each end saying 'Sorry, please go on.'

This was a lesson that had to be learnt in the early days of satellite broadcasting which became more acute when digital processing and encoding was introduced – yet you still see these problems occurring today.

MPEG picture problems

Audio compression

Audio compression is aimed at dealing with both speech and music signals in a perceptual manner.

A perceptual audio coder does not attempt to accurately reconstruct the input signal after encoding and decoding, rather its goal is to ensure that the output signal sounds the same to the listener.

The primary psychoacoustic effect that the perceptual audio coder uses is called auditory masking, where parts of a signal which are not discernible by the human ear can be imperceptibly removed.

Psychoacoustics

Psychoacoustics plays a key role by compressing parts of the signal that are imperceptible to the human ear.

The human ear hears frequencies between 20 Hz and 20 kHz, and the human voice typically produces sounds in the range of 400 Hz–4 kHz, with the ear most sensitive in the range of 2–4 kHz.

The low frequencies are vowels and bass, while the high frequencies are consonants. The dynamic range (i.e. quietest to loudest sounds) of the human ear is about 96 dB (around four thousand million to one), with the threshold of pain at around 115 dBA and permanent damage at around 130 dBA. The dBA is a unit of measurement of the sound pressure level that the ear is sensitive to.

It could be considered that audio does not need to be compressed as it uses relatively little bandwidth compared to video.

CD audio, for instance, is not compressed, and has 44 100 samples per second (44.1 kHz sampling), with 16 bits per sample and 2 channels (stereo), which gives a data rate of 1.4 Mbps.

It can also be argued (and hotly by audiophiles!) that audio suffers when it is compressed. However, it is both desirable and possible to compress the audio signal with no discernibly detrimental effect to reduce the overall data rate of the programme signal.

There are several techniques for the real-time digitization and compression of audio signals, some having been defined as international standards, and some remain proprietary systems (e.g. Dolby AC-3).

Audio sampling and masking

The processes used in digital audio compression are in principle the same as in digital video compression.

In the psychoacoustic model, the human ear appears to be more discerning than the human eye, which only requires a relatively limited dynamic range of dark to light. Because of the higher resolution required for audio due to the greater sensitivity of the human ear, the audio is typically sampled with 16 bits per sample. The typical sampling frequencies for audio are 32, 44.1 or 48 kHz.

After quantization the coded bit stream has a range of rates typically from 32 to 384 kbps.

In order to achieve higher compression ratios and transmit wider bandwidth of audio, MPEG audio compression uses in particular a technique known as 'masking'.

Imagine a musical ensemble comprising several different instruments and playing all at the same time. The human ear is not capable of hearing all of the components of the sound because some of the quieter sounds are hidden or masked by the louder sounds.

If a recording was made of the music and the parts that we could not hear were removed, we would still hear the same sound, but we would have recorded much less data. This is exactly the way in which audio compression works, by removing the parts of the sound that we could not hear in any case.

Audio compression

Digital modulation in SNG

Without going into heavy-duty theory, you need to appreciate that there are different types of modulation (we have already gone over the basics of this) and in digital modulation the predominant modulation is QPSK – a type of phase modulation. Other types of phase modulation are 8-PSK and 16QAM, but these are not commonly used in DSNG.

With QPSK, the carrier undergoes four changes in phase and can thus represent 4 bits of data, and every 2 bits in a QPSK modulated signal make up a 'symbol'. We talk of a digital modulated signal in symbols per second, or mega (million) symbols per second (MSps).

We have talked about encoding in terms of compression and MPEG-2, but there is also an element of digital encoding within the digital modulation process.

This is because bits are added in the modulation of a digital signal to correct for errors in transmission – termed 'error correction'.

The signal is inevitably degraded in transmission due to the effects of noise and interference, and to compensate for this inevitable consequence, 'check' bits are added to the bit stream in the modulator to enable errors to be detected at the downlink.

Error correction

Although error correction coding reduces the transmission power required, as the error correction can tolerate higher levels of unwanted signal (noise), the demand for bandwidth increases because of the greater overall amount of data being transmitted.

There are two types of error correction added to the digital stream in its transmission to correct for errors – Reed–Solomon and forward error correction.

In Reed–Solomon code, each block of data of programme signal has an additional check block of data added to compensate for any errors that the signal may suffer on its passage from the transmitter to the receiver. In a data stream used in a DSNG uplink, the Reed–Solomon code is defined as (204,188).

The second error correction process is forward error correction (FEC), where bits are added in a predetermined pattern. This is decoded at the receiver using a decoding process called Viterbi to detect any loss of information bits, and attempt to reconstruct the missing ones.

The number of bits added by this process defines the FEC ratio for the signal, and is typically 3/4 – in other words, for each 3 bits, 1 extra bit has been added. Some of the other FEC rates for QPSK that can be used are 1/2, 2/3 and 5/6 but the standard DSNG rate is generally 3/4.

The greater the degree of FEC applied, the more rugged the signal will become, but the occupied bandwidth will need to increase to cope with the error correction overhead. Occupied bandwidth is – as the name suggests – the amount of bandwidth that the signal occupies.

Transmission and symbol rates

The overall data rate, including RS, FEC and the information rate is termed the Transmission Rate. So now we can calculate the actual transmitted symbol rate – this is an important defining parameter for a digital signal.

If we assume that a typical DSNG signal is an 8 Mbps information rate signal, then this is an actual bit-rate of 8.448 Mbps – a standard data rate in the digital 'hierarchy'. The data stream is QPSK modulated, so the information symbol rate is 4.224 MSps (2 bits per symbol), and the calculations produce a transmitted symbol rate of 6.1113 MSps.

Therefore, the 8 Mbps DSNG signal is expressed as an 8.448 Mbps signal transmitted with QPSK modulation at 3/4 FEC rate, and 204,188 Reed–Solomon coding, giving a modulated symbol rate (Modulation Rate) of 6.1113 MSps.

Sometimes the transmitted symbol rate is expressed without RS coding, which in this case is 5.632 MSps.

The RF bandwidth required is approximately the Modulation Rate multiplied by a factor – typically 1.35 – to give the occupied bandwidth. This signal will fit within a 9 MHz channel – it will actually occupy just over 8 MHz, but there is a guard band allowed, minimizing any interference with signals in adjacent channels on the satellite.

The 9 MHz channel has become a nominal standard for DSNG signals in most satellite operators' systems.

Quality and compression

Video compression is widespread in broadcasting, and a very large proportion of SNG operations are now in the digital domain. The effect of compression on picture content varies widely depending on that content, and there is still no widely accepted scientific method of measuring picture quality – the human eye has been found to be the best guide, but it is a subjective evaluation.

However, suffice to say that for most news organizations, the advantages of the cost of utilizing compression far outweigh what are considered esoteric concerns over issues of quality.

An inevitable result of compression, whether video or audio, is delay. There are a number of computations carried out in both the compression and decompression processes, and the higher order compression processes (such as MPEG-2) take longer to be completed than the more simpler compression systems. However, as we have seen, there are ways to minimize the on-screen effects of this.

DSNG processing equipment

In our look at the various types of equipment in the uplink, we need to give an idea of the sizes of the units. Equipment is typically not in stand-alone cases, but designed to be screwed into equipment racks or bays.

There is an internationally recognized way of measuring the height and width of equipment – the Rack Unit (RU). The rack width is defined as 19 inches (and hence 'half rack' width is, as it suggests, 9½ inches wide), and 1 RU is equal to 1.75 inches (44.5 mm) high (incidentally there is no standard for the depth of equipment).

Encoders

As we have seen, a digital compression encoder essentially converts full bandwidth (uncompressed) video and audio to a compressed digital signal, and then the output is connected to the upconverter.

We have also seen that the digital compression standard used for DSNG and DENG is MPEG-2. The encoder has analogue or serial digital video (SDI) and audio inputs, with some degree of input level control.

There are also front panel controls for setting a number of digital parameters:

- bit-rate of video and audio sampling
- symbol rate
- horizontal and vertical resolution
- delay mode.

The typical bit-rate for DSNG is 8 Mbps (this is known as the information rate), although there is a move to lower information rates as quality improves with advances in technology.

The output is produced as a multiplexed video and audio DVB compliant signal that can then be fed to the modulator. This is also referred to as ASI standard (Asynchronous Serial Interface).

MPEG-2 encoders designed specifically for DSNG are typically only 1 RU high.

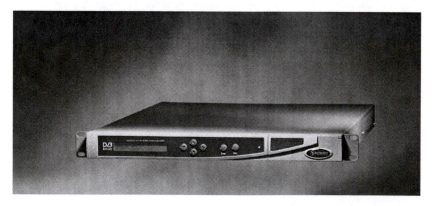

MPEG encoder/modulator (© Scopus Network Technologies)

Modulator (modem)

The modulator in a digital SNG system is often referred to as a DVB modulator, as it requires a DVB ASI standard input, with the incoming signal containing the compressed video and audio programme information.

The modulator will typically have the following front panel controls:

- Modulation scheme – QPSK, 8-PSK, 16QAM
- FEC rate – 1/2, 2/3, 3/4, etc.
- Data rate
- Output carrier frequency – usually 70 MHz or at L-band
- Carrier on/off – this is the pure carrier before modulation is added
- Output level control – the final level of the signal.

The Reed–Solomon error code settings are set (204,188), and are not user-configurable.

The output is produced as a signal modulated onto an IF carrier signal as we have already seen in DENG.

There are several MPEG encoder/modulators on the market that combine the encoder and the modulator in a single unit, typically 2 RU or even 1 RU high. These units are just as functional as separate units, but have been designed with the size and space restraints of DSNG in mind.

Modulator (© SWEDISH Satellite Systems AB)

Upconverters

The function of the upconverter is to transform the modulated IF signal from the modulator up to the desired Ku-band frequency by a process of frequency shifting or conversion.

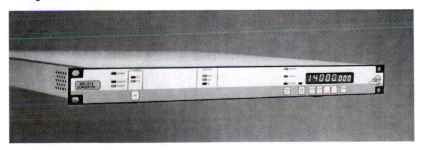

Upconverter (© Advent Communications Ltd)

DSNG processing equipment

The upconverter, typically a 1 RU unit, usually has few controls on it, the most significant of which is the upconverter output frequency.

Assuming the next stage of upconversion is a fixed frequency transition, then this frequency control is usually calibrated in the final Ku-band frequency. Therefore, this is effectively the equipment on which the operator 'dials-up' the actual transmit frequency.

The output of this first stage of upconversion then passes to the fixed upconverter. This unit may either be rack-mounted, or if mounted as near as possible to the HPA to minimize losses is normally contained within a small weather-proofed box.

The final upconverter produces a low-level Ku-band 'drive' signal that is applied to the HPA, which then amplifies this to the desired transmit level.

Amplifiers

High power amplifiers (HPA) for digital SNG use typically range in size from 100 to 300 W. The function of the HPA is to amplify the low-level signal from the upconverter to a very large power that is then fed to the antenna.

At the heart of the HPA is a device called a travelling wave tube (TWT), which is essentially a very powerful amplifying vacuum tube, and is relatively fragile.

Although the output power of the HPA is measured in Watts, it is often expressed in dB Watts, or dBW. Where a single programme signal is being uplinked, this mode of operation is termed single channel per carrier (SCPC), and applies to both analogue and digital operation.

If there are multiple carriers being combined and uplinked, this is termed multiple carriers per channel (MCPC).

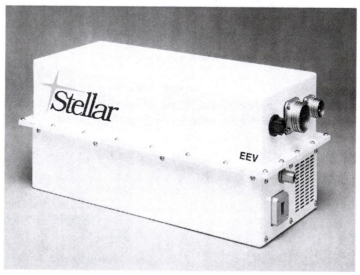

(a)

HPA units (© E2V Technologies Ltd)

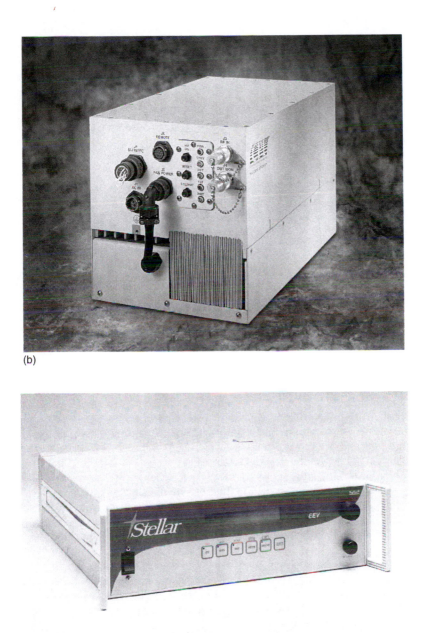

(b)

(c)

HPA units   continued

(d)

HPA units continued

The output power of an uplink is defined by two parameters – the output power of the HPA and the gain of the antenna. The output power of the HPA is often referred to as the 'flange' power, which is the power delivered to the output port flange (connector) of the amplifier.

The connections throughout the system so far have been with coaxial cable, but the connection from the HPA to the antenna uses a waveguide.

Waveguide is a specially formed hollow metal tube, rectangular in cross-section (and often referred to as 'plumbing' for obvious reasons), which is manufactured with differing degrees of mechanical flexibility (rigid, semi-rigid or flexible).

It is vital that the connections of waveguide joints are as effective as possible, as microwave signals leak very easily from an incorrectly made joint. In particular, it must be noted that the power levels are hazardous, and you need to fully appreciate the hazards and the necessary safety measures, so we will be looking at these in more detail later.

HPAs are generally packaged in one of two different ways – either as an antenna-mount (hub-mount) or as a rack-mount. Hub-mount HPAs are usually in the lower power range – 50–200 W – and are typically used in DSNG because of the smaller power required.

The hub-mounted HPA is mounted very close to or actually on the dish assembly (hence the name). The advantage of mounting it in such a fashion is that the power losses in the waveguide connection between the HPA output flange and the antenna feedhorn are minimized because of the short physical length of the waveguide connection.

The rack-mounted HPA is, as the name suggests, mounted more remotely from the antenna in an equipment rack, in either a flyaway or vehicle installation, and is offered in a higher range of output powers.

DSNG processing equipment

SNG antennas

We now come to the focal point of the uplink – the antenna. The function of the antenna is to take the signal from the HPA and both further amplify the signal and focus the beam towards the satellite. Although there are a wide variety of antennas used in satellite communications, SNG uplink systems always use a parabolic type, similar to what we saw earlier in terrestrial ENG microwave. Downlink reception systems also use parabolic antennas.

We have already looked at the characteristics of parabolic (dish) antennas earlier in considering terrestrial microwave, so what are the differences seen in an SNG dish?

To recap, a parabolic surface produces a parallel beam of energy if the surface is illuminated at its focus, and the parabolic dish is commonly referred to as the reflector. The signal is transmitted via the feedhorn assembly on the antenna, and this is often loosely referred to as the waveguide, feed or 'launcher' (as it 'launches' the signal).

The parabolic antenna family has a wide number of variants, but the types used for SNG systems are primarily the 'prime focus' and 'offset prime focus' types.

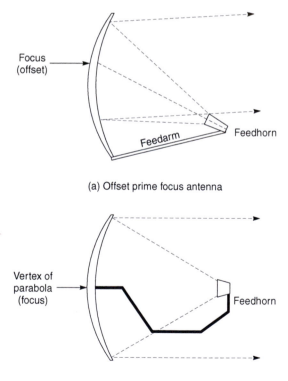

(a) Offset prime focus antenna

(b) In-line prime focus antenna

Antenna types

108

A parabolic antenna is fundamentally described by two parameters. The physical diameter of the antenna is expressed in metres, and the amplification factor (gain) of the antenna is measured in dBi.

The construction of the antenna varies according to the application, varying depending on whether it is to be used in a flyaway or is mounted on a vehicle as we shall look at later. All antennas now have to meet the requirement of being able to operate to satellites spaced only 2° apart in the geostationary arc. The reason for the demand for 2° spacing is that in the 1980s it was anticipated that the number of satellites was going to steadily increase, with a resulting need to move satellites closer together to increase capacity in the geostationary arc.

This means not interfering with satellites adjacent to the intended one, and therefore the radiation pattern from the antenna has to be accurately defined.

The gain figure is the single most important descriptor of the antenna, as together with the power output rating of the HPA, the total system power is defined by adding the HPA dBW figure to the dBi figure from the antenna. This gives us a measurement called the Effective Isotropic Radiated Power (EIRP).

As an example – and this might look a bit complicated but it is necessary to look at it – a 180 W HPA produces 22 dBW, and a 1.5 m antenna has a gain of 45 dBi, and by adding these two figures together we have a maximum system EIRP of 67 dBW – a typical uplink power requirement for a Ku-band DSNG system. Normally the system does not need to run at maximum theoretical power (and it can cause a few problems), and the typical amount of power for a DSNG uplink to work on the current generation of satellites is below 60 dBW (which is significantly less). It can be complicated measuring in dBs, as they are not a linear measurement, so for our purposes here, this is as far as we need to go. However, as a comparison, analogue SNG systems would typically need over twice this amount of power (near to 70 dBW).

Feedhorn polarization

Earlier we discussed the property of polarization. As we saw earlier in terrestrial ENG microwave, the two types of polarization – circular and linear – are each further subdivided, and determine how the signal is transmitted from the feed-horn. A signal uplinked on one particular polarization is typically downlinked on the opposite polarization. Ku-band signals are generally linearly polarized, while C-band signals are often circularly polarized – but there are exceptions.

On both the uplink and the downlink, the feedhorn is additionally rotated to compensate for the angular difference between the antenna position on the Earth's surface and the satellite position. This is referred to as polarization 'skew', and the degree of skew can be calculated from the latitude and longitude of the uplink (or downlink). Particularly for linear polarization, it is critical in achieving a good transmission or reception of a signal that the polarization skew is correctly applied to the antenna.

It is also important that any receive antenna is as 'blind' as possible to signals on the opposite polarization – this is termed cross-polar discrimination (XPD) – so that any potential interference from a signal on the same frequency but opposite polarization is minimized.

Link budgets

The fundamental basis for assessing whether a satellite link will work is the calculation of the link budget. This determines how much signal transmitted from the uplink will arrive at the downlink, and hopefully with enough in hand to give some degree of margin for physical factors that can vary or cannot be calculated in a theoretical link budget.

What are we trying to measure with the calculation of a link budget?

Fundamentally, whether enough signal transmitted from the uplink can be received at the downlink to convey the information carried accurately. This encompasses the uplink and the downlink equipment, the uplink and the downlink paths, as well as the effects of the reception and transmission through the satellite.

The link budget is similar to a financial budget, with contributions (income) and deductions (expenditure) that define the overall performance, where the currency is the decibel (dB). As with a financial budget calculation, depending on the level of detail, the link budget can be a relatively simple one, involving perhaps only a page of calculations, or it can be extremely detailed, and spread over up to ten pages.

Digital link budgets are complex, due to the potential effects of interference from both adjacent signals and natural sources of interference.

The significant results of the link budget will be ratios that are a measure of the predicted quality of the link.

First there is the Eb/No (pronounced 'ebbno') – which defines how much energy has been received in each bit compared to the background noise. It describes how good the link is.

A 'good' link will have an Eb/No of at least 7 or 8, and hopefully as high as 12 or 13. On the other hand, an Eb/No of 5 or 6 is marginal, and the link is likely to fail.

Secondly, there is the bit error rate (BER – pronounced 'berr'), which is the ratio of bits received in error compared to the total number of bits sent.

Again, it is an indicator of how good the link is, so a BER of 10^{-6} is good (i.e. there is only one error in every million bits), whereas a BER of 10^{-3} is very marginal (where there is an error in every 1000 bits).

Both the Eb/No and the BER are interrelated, so if the Eb/No is too low (and hence the BER is too high) the decoder at the downlink will suddenly stop working, giving a frozen or black picture.

The calculation of a link budget enables us to predict to a given degree how good (or bad) the link will actually perform. In practice, the results will be disappointing, if:

- the uplink does not produce enough power
- the satellite does not have a sensitive enough receive characteristic
- the satellite does not have a powerful enough transmit characteristic
- the downlink antenna is not large enough (and therefore does not have enough gain)
- there is more noise and interference than expected.

With a digital link, anything apart from total success results in just nothing at all. Digital signals suffer from what is known as the 'cliff-edge' effect – that is, either perfect results, or no pictures and sound.

What prevents the signal being clearly received?

Assuming that the uplink and the downlink equipment are working correctly, then it is predominantly the factors of interference, noise and losses, such as the scattering of the signal as it travels through space and the atmosphere on both the uplink and the downlink paths.

Calculating link budgets manually is extremely time consuming, and it is common for uplink operators to use software packages such as Arrowe Satmaster Pro, which calculates not only the link budget but also produces pointing data (azimuth, elevation, etc.).

Fade margin

As we saw in our discussion in terrestrial microwave links, the difference between the operating level of the link and the point at which it fails because the power level reaching the receiver is too low is called the fade margin. This is usually calculated as part of the link budget. The fade margin is expressed in dB.

DSNG uplink types

An SNG uplink system consists of the following primary component parts:

- antenna with mounting support
- high power amplifier(s) (HPA)
- upconverter
- modulator
- signal monitoring
- baseband signal processing.

The physical transmission components of an uplink are typically referred to collectively as the chain or thread. A chain typically consists of a single transmission path that has one of each of the primary transmission components – digital encoder, modulator, upconverter and an HPA.

An SNG system may have some or all of its constituent components duplicated – two or more chains can be combined to feed via a single antenna, using a phase-combiner.

This may be to give a degree of redundancy and provide immediate back-up in the event of failure, or an extra HPA may be added to increase the uplink power (not usual in digital systems).

It may be that the system has to provide more than one transmission path where there is a requirement to uplink more than one programme signal simultaneously, combining two programme signals into a single signal applied to the antenna. A single transmission chain could also achieve this by using cascaded digital encoders.

There are several different configurations that can be used, but no matter what the configuration, in news operations the factors of speed and reliability are significant issues, and the component parts have to be rugged, reliable and quick to set up in operation.

However, as might be guessed from what has already been said, a system can be configured in a variety of ways. The characteristics of an SNG system are defined by:

- type of packaging – e.g. vehicle or flyaway
- frequency band of operation – C- or Ku-Band
- level of redundancy – none, partial or full
- number of *paths* – one, two or more.

By their very nature, SNG systems are not permanently fixed as the essential requirement is to be able to move quickly and operate in response to a breaking news story.

SNG systems therefore have to be packaged in a way that allows them to be easily transported and then rapidly set up on location.

Configuration

Systems are constructed in either one of the following ways:

- Flyaways – As indicated by the term, flyaway systems are designed to be broken down to fit into a number of equipment cases for easy transportation by air and then reassembled on location.
- Vehicle based – the SNG uplink is typically built into a vehicle (a van or a truck) as a permanent installation. The system can then be driven to location and quickly put into operation.

DSNG uplink types

Flyaways

Flyaway systems fulfil a primary requirement for a system that can be easily transported by air and reassembled at location in typically under an hour – a flyaway can even be rigged and operated out of the back of an ordinary box-body truck.

The flexibility of flyaways in ease of transportation is of critical value to international newsgatherers, who regularly fly all over the world with such systems in a variety of sizes and types of aircraft.

The key factors are total weight and number of cases, as news crews frequently transport these systems on scheduled commercial flights as excess baggage. Costs consequently increase greatly in direct proportion to weight and volume.

The design of a flyaway has diametrically opposed demands. Strength has to be achieved with minimum mass while also sustaining stability. Precision and adherence to close mechanical tolerances have to be met while all components have to be rugged.

Overall size has to be minimized while also achieving maximum uplink power. The individual component parts have to be in an easily assembled form for both minimum rigging time and reliable operation.

Either the antenna is transported in a single piece or it is broken down into a number of segments or petals. It can then be mechanically reassembled on-site onto the support or mount system, which has to be achieved to a very high tolerance.

The antenna has to be mounted so that it can easily be steered to align to the satellite correctly. Yet at the same time, the mount has to provide maximum rigidity and stability to maintain pointing accuracy up to the satellite during operation even in poor weather.

However, this physical rigidity has to be achieved while keeping the mass (and therefore weight) of both the mount and the antenna to the minimum. The use of carbon fibre and aluminium alloys is common to achieve these design aims.

The control of the antenna is a very precise engineering requirement. The antenna has to be able to be finely adjusted in three axes – azimuth, elevation and polarization, as shown in the figure opposite.

Azimuth (the rotational position), elevation (the angle of tilt) and polarization (the circular orientation of the beam) all have to be controlled to within fractions of a degree.

There are typically both coarse and fine adjustment controls provided on the mount to achieve this.

The coarse controls allow rapid movement of the antenna to a point very close to the desired position, while the fine controls allow precise final alignment of the antenna towards the satellite.

When the antenna has been aligned, it is critically important that the antenna remains on-station, as once it is correctly positioned, it must be positively locked in position so that it cannot then be knocked off alignment accidentally or by bad weather.

Manufacturers use different techniques to achieve stability, based either around simple tripods, complex stabilizing frames and legs, or even interlocking

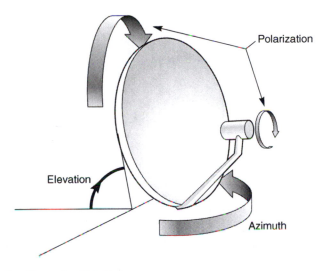

Azimuth, elevation and polarization

the antenna and mount to equipment cases to increase the ground footprint of the system.

The antenna must also be capable of being positioned on uneven ground and retaining pointing accuracy under quite severe weather conditions such as high winds.

In aerodynamic terms, the antenna represents a sailplane, so it is important to bear in mind that there is a maximum survival wind speed as a measurement of stability in poor conditions.

Antennas

The antenna itself in a flyaway system is typically between 0.9 and 2.2 m, and as previously mentioned it is also usually segmented to allow easy transportation.

Only the smallest antennas (1 m or under) can easily be shipped as a single piece assembly. Antennas are usually either circular or diamond-shaped (or even a flattened diamond-shape) though the smaller antennas are typically circular, as shown in the following pages 115 and 116.

Flight-cases

The remainder of the system consists of a number of cases of electronic equipment where the equipment is grouped in a manner to keep the number of cases to a minimum but also allow easy manual handling.

Typically, the electronic equipment is fitted into flight-cases. This grouping also has to match the functionality of the system, so that the component parts that directly electrically interconnect are also next to each other, particularly for high-power RF signals.

(a)

1.5 m Flyaway antenna ((a) © SWE DISH Satellite Systems AB)

A flight-case is essentially a case that has an outer skin of (usually) metal while the contents are in some way protected against mechanical shock. This shock protection is high-density foam for the antenna and mount elements, and sprung-mounted frames for the electronics.

An equipment flight-case has an internal shockproof-mounted frame into which the electronics are fitted in such a way as to allow quick and easy set-up for operation at the destination. The removable front cover allows access to the front control panel, and typically has neoprene seals to protect ingress of water and dirt during transit.

The rear of the case may also be removable to allow access to rear panel connectors and controls. A flight-case typically costs several thousand dollars, and this may seem very high until the cost of the equipment it is designed

(b)

2.4 m Flyaway antenna ((b) © GigaSat Ltd)

to protect is taken into account – which can be typically ten times the cost of the case.

The case also has to be able to allow the equipment inside to operate satisfactorily in extremes of temperature, high humidity, driving rain, or standing in shallow puddles.

Some cases are also designed to minimize the effects of any external electromagnetic interference (EMI). Taking into account all these factors, it is easy to see why the cases are so expensive.

Nonetheless, the fact that the cases are so rugged does not mean that the usual standards of care in handling delicate electronic equipment can be neglected.

If care is taken in handling as well as the use of these cases, the equipment should be fully operational when it reaches its destination.

The baseband equipment provided with an SNG uplink can vary widely, from simple monitoring of the incoming video to providing a small OB facility. This may include vision switcher, routing matrix, one or more equipped camera positions and comprehensive studio-remote communications.

Flight cased system (© GigaSat Ltd)

Typical flyaway operation

Because there is such a wide variation of situations for flyaway operations, it is perhaps most useful to look at a particular scenario.

Let us imagine that the story is a major international one; for example, in the aftermath of the attacks on New York and Washington of 11 September 2001. During the US reprisals against Afghanistan, there was a major newsgathering presence in Pakistan. All the major TV networks were there, and there was a considerable presence in Islamabad and Peshawar in Pakistan.

A typical operation would have been based at a hotel. Four or five star international chain hotels offer a number of benefits for flyaway operations – there are often extensive grounds or roof areas for the rigging of the flyaway antennas, the crews can stay as well as work in the hotel, and additional rooms can easily be acquired for all the operational activities.

Most of all, in a hostile situation international hotels are often the safest places to be.

Supposing that this operation is rigged at a hotel, then the uplink will probably be on the roof with a power generator.

Although local power from the hotel is available and used, it is usual to back this up with your own source of power. The most common requirement is to be able to do stand-up 'lives' and replay tape material.

This means providing a live camera position, with studio-remote communications and some audio mixing for the reporter and perhaps a guest contributor, and also a VTR to play in material live or feed back to the studio for later transmission.

There needs to be a small routing switcher, able to synchronously switch (i.e. with no picture roll or glitch) between the output of the camera and the VTR, and some vision and sound monitoring.

The edit suite can be several floors below in a room, while the 'live' position may be on the roof or on a room balcony, to give a visual background statement of the location of the story. The switching/monitoring point is likely to be in another hotel room, which often doubles up as a production office.

One of the problems faced in these situations is the amount of signal cabling required.

The cabling requirements are quite considerable, particularly if there is a significant distance between the stand-up live camera position, the edit suite, the switching/monitoring point and the satellite uplink. All too quickly the interconnection requirements can rise to the extent that there may be perhaps over 100 kg of cable alone to be transported to cover hundreds of metres of multiple interconnects.

Let us look at each of the parts of this operation in a little more detail. Many aspects of the operation are identical to what is necessary with a terrestrial ENG microwave operation – because the only thing that is different is the transmission medium.

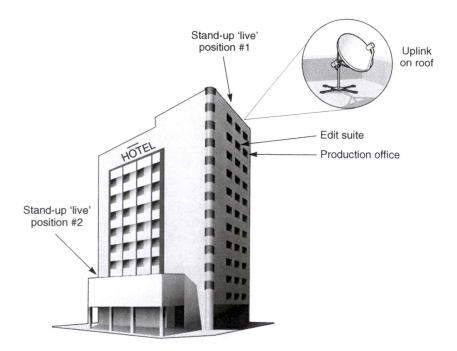

Stand-up 'live' position #1

Uplink on roof

Edit suite

Production office

HOTEL

Stand-up 'live' position #2

Hotel scenario

Live position

The live position needs to 'say' something about the story. It could be that for safety or practical reasons the live position cannot be in the place where you would ideally like it to be, but nevertheless you have to pick as good a position as possible.

Often the producer or reporter will decide where the live position should be, but hopefully they will get the opinion from the technicians as to the feasibility of its situation. The background has to 'set the scene', perhaps with a well-known landmark – but often you do not have that luxury.

Wherever it is, it has to be safe and practical to work from. You may be squashed up with three other live positions of other broadcasters, so you just have to make the best of it and obtain a decent shot for the news editor.

Studio-remote communications

Communications with the studio in SNG operations always involve comms circuits such as two-way talkback (4-wire) and IFB.

Other communication circuits will include a number of telephone lines and a data connection with the newsroom computer system.

These can all be provided either via an additional transmit/receive equipment on the satellite uplink (sometimes referred to as commslink), via an Inmarsat satphone (we will look at these later), or via any available telephone landlines.

The most desirable method of delivery is via the satellite uplink, as this usually provides the most direct paths to and from the studio.

The connection to the newsroom computer system and the provision of multiple telephone circuits are critical. The integration of the newsroom computer system into the overall news production process means that it acts as the heart of both the newsgathering and the news output operation. Information regarding contacts, running orders, news agency wire information and background information to the story are all controlled and produced by the newsroom computer system, as well as providing rapid messaging between the editorial staff and the field staff. It is also a fact that there can never be too many telephones – you will always have someone needing to make calls!

No matter how simple the operation, however, this aspect of the news broadcasting chain is vital. Many operations have failed not for lack of programme pictures and sound, but because the studio-remote communications have not been working correctly.

Commslink

The provision of IFB, talkback, telephone circuits, and the connection to the newsroom computer system can all be provided via an additional transmit/receive side-chain on the satellite uplink. The comms is uplinked as a separate carrier in the same frequency band as the main programme uplink channel, and is typically at a data rate of 64 kbps – hence it is common to talk of comms 'channels' in terms of 64 kbps slots.

The comms carrier does not need to be transmitted at as high a power level as the main programme signal, because of the much smaller bandwidth requirement of the data carrier of the comms. It is combined with the main outgoing programme signal just before the HPA.

If it is a simple comms system, with just a single audio 'go' and 'return' for IFB, then the signals can be sent and received via a comms modem. For a more complex system, a 'statistical' data multiplexer is used that can vary the allocation of the relatively narrow data bandwidth of each of the audio channels according to the wider simultaneous bandwidth demand of a number of circuits.

The use of an integrated communications system with the uplink is highly advantageous, from both a cost and a convenience point of view, as the bandwidth and power requirements of the comms carriers on the transponder are much lower than for the main programme channel, and hence much cheaper.

Video editing

In addition, it is often a requirement to provide a video editing facility at the uplink location, and if this edit suite is required to be a source to the routing switcher as well, then this will further complicate the system.

The format of the video editing varies according to the organization, but Sony SX and Panasonic's DVCPro digital tape formats are replacing the once dominant older analogue Sony BetaSP format. DVCam, originally intended only as a domestic format, is also increasingly in use as a budget newsgathering format.

Typical flyaway operation

The appeal of the digital formats in the field are the compact laptop editors, weighing under 10 kg, which considerably reduce the average 150 kg of equipment that traditionally made up a BetaSP edit pack.

Whatever the format of the video editing, it is common to try to provide the ability to connect the editing as an online facility to the rest of the rig. This is so that an edited piece (a cut) that has just been finished can be immediately played out on the satellite uplink, without the necessity to take the tape to a separate VTR for playout.

Electrical power

Because mains power may not be available or if it is, may not be very reliable, a power generator is required as well. Because some of the live-shots may take place at night or under bright sun, either of which will require additional lighting for the live stand-up position, the generator will need to be capable of delivering suitable levels of power.

The uplink system itself may require quite a significant amount of power, so the generator (or generators) will need to supply typically somewhere between 5 and 20 kW, depending on the overall demand.

Generators are one of the most common reasons for failures in the operation of SNG uplink systems. There is a maxim that a generator will always fail (it is just a matter of when) as they are notoriously unreliable – not helped by the less than ideal conditions they are often operated in.

The challenges

On covering a story like this, it is critical to get to the location and rig as fast as possible. The whole system has to be built, tested and be operational in typically about 12–18 hours from arrival on location – and that does not include getting through the Customs formalities and travelling from the airport.

All these elements also mean that the total number of cases that make up the entire system as we have discussed will probably double or triple the number of cases that make up the basic SNG uplink alone.

The truth is that to mount an operation as described above, there is likely to be a total of 40–50 cases, and the total weight of the cases between 1000 and 1500 kg (see opposite).

With the new 'lightweight' DSNG systems, this shipped weight can be reduced, but perhaps not as dramatically as might be assumed. Although there are complete lightweight SNG flyaway systems that claim to have a shipping weight near to 250 kg, production demands can quickly increase this weight.

This in turn can mean that the system described above has to be expanded to meet this greater demand, and the net result can be just as much equipment has to be provided.

However, it is possible with determination – both technical and editorial – to 'travel light' and to keep the amount of equipment required under 600 kg, and on certain stories this may be essential for logistical and safety reasons.

Typical SNG flyaway system – packaged to go!

Often on this type of story there will be other staff engaged locally – 'fixers', translators, drivers, etc.

A fixer is someone who has a good deal of local knowledge, and as the name suggests, be able to 'fix' things from finding and making the contacts for interviews, to liasing with local officials to make sure the whole operation runs as smoothly as possible.

SNG vehicles

SNG vehicles can be built on a variety of types of base vehicles such as towed trailers, estate cars, SUV/MPVs, pick-up vehicles, panel vans, box-body vehicles and even combined tractor units for towing production trailers.

However, in Europe the majority of SNG vehicles, sometimes referred to as satellite newsgathering vehicles (SNVs), are constructed on panel vans weighing between 3500 and 7500 kg. Some of the following explanations also apply to ENG microwave vehicles, particularly the means of providing electrical power.

The primary purpose of an SNV is to allow operational deployment to be accomplished more quickly than with a flyaway, and to have a number of additional facilities to be built-in so that they are also rapidly available once on-site.

These facilities typically include an on-board generator to provide electrical power, baseband signal production, signal routing, and bidirectional studio-remote communications.

One of the principal characteristics of achieving fast deployment is, of course, having the antenna already mounted on the vehicle. The antenna can be controlled so that it can be pointed at the satellite from the comfort of the vehicle interior. It is common to have an antenna that is mounted on the roof and which is motorized for remotely adjusting azimuth, elevation and polarization.

The SNV has a number of sub-systems fitted to it beyond the basic satellite uplink system, so in addition it usually has the following installed:

- electrical power generator system
- stabilizing jacking system
- installed broadcast equipment.

Electrical power generator

Whereas a flyaway relies on power being provided from somewhere else, either from a building supply or from a separate generator, the SNG truck, depending on the size of the vehicle, usually has one of the following three types of electrical system:

- Self-contained generator driven by an engine separate from the vehicle road engine.
- Inverter system, where the road engine drives a 12 V/24 V alternator which then supplies 115 V/230 V via an inverter.
- Power take-off systems (PTO) where the road engine drives a generator either via a belt or indirectly via a specially equipped vehicle gearbox.

As with powering flyaways, it should be noted that whichever type of power system is used, the whole area of electrical power on location is fraught with difficulties. The power supply to the uplink from whatever type of generating system is likely to fail at some point, and some (wise) uplink operators have taken to having two sources available on a vehicle, with one acting as a standby emergency source. The reason for the likelihood of failure is, as we have already pointed out, generators are notoriously unreliable because of the less than ideal conditions they are often operated in.

There is also a potential safety issue where power is provided from an external input instead of from the on-board generator – often referred to as 'shore-power'.

The condition of the incoming supply cannot be necessarily known, and it is usual to provide protection by use of a residual current device (RCD) which will turn off the power in the event of an electrical fault on the vehicle.

An RCD operates by sensing when the current in the live and neutral supply are not equal and opposite. Any imbalance is usually due to a path to earth due to excessive leakage and/or a fault situation.

Stabilizing jacking system

The vehicle usually requires a stabilizing jacking system to ensure that the antenna stays 'on station', as any movement of the vehicle could result in the movement of the antenna.

Movement of the vehicle can result from either people getting in and out or wind rocking the vehicle (e.g. if the wind is coming broadside onto the vehicle or from other vehicles passing by at high speed). It is common to provide either a two- or four-point stabilizing system, with either two jacks at each rear corner of the vehicle, two at the middle of the vehicle on each side, or four jacks, one at each corner.

The jacks can be manually, electrically or hydraulically operated. The most sophisticated stabilizing systems have computer-controlled stabilizing of the vehicle, with an on-board sensor feeding back the status of vehicle stability.

Manual systems are usually fitted to smaller lower cost vehicles, but the time taken to prepare the vehicle for operation is slower. It is possible on some vehicles not to have any stabilization if the antenna is small, as having a wider beamwidth than larger antennas, a slight movement of the antenna will not move it off-station.

Level of redundancy

Redundancy gives protection against failure of part of the system, and is an important factor to consider if the system is being used to cover an important event or story.

An SNG system may have part or all of its electronic equipment duplicated to give a degree of redundancy. Normally it is not necessary to duplicate any of the mechanical components, save for perhaps having a spare length of flexible waveguide that interconnects the HPA to the antenna.

The level of redundancy can be varied according to the requirement. It might perhaps be sufficient to add a second HPA and upconverter – this would give partial redundancy.

To achieve greater redundancy another modulator should be added. The additional HPA can either be combined with the primary HPA via a phase-combiner, or made available as a hot-spare via a waveguide switch.

A hot-spare is a part of the system which is switched on and in a fully operational state ready for rapid changeover in the event of a failure – conversely, a cold-spare is not switched on and ready! Additionally for a digital system, it might be decided that the digital modulator and the encoder should be replicated to achieve full redundancy.

The decision as to what level of redundancy is required or desired is not an easy one. In such a complex array of equipment as an SNG system, failures are inevitable at some point during the system's life, and even full redundancy can never remove that risk totally – it simply minimizes it. Companies that hire SNG systems to broadcasters regard higher levels of redundancy as a priority so that the exposure of risk of failure to their clients is minimized.

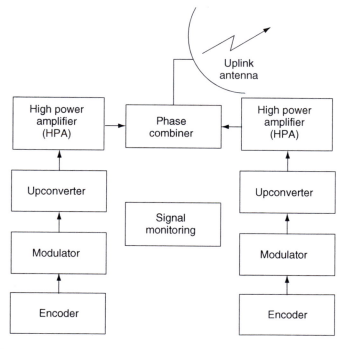

Redundancy

Other organizations, particularly the global broadcasters who are primarily servicing their own outlets, prefer to reduce the capital cost, size and weight of the system and work with minimal redundancy, willing to take the risk of an occasional failure in return for a lower capital cost and lower revenue costs in shipping smaller flyaway systems around the world.

Multiple programme paths

It is now a common requirement to provide more than one programme path from a single SNG link. This may be to provide differing sources of material to the destination simultaneously, either off-tape or 'live', or to service different destinations simultaneously.

For whatever reason, there are two methods of providing multiple paths. One is to provide two separate uplink chains that are combined just before the input to the antenna – this is the 'RF solution'.

The second method can only be achieved with a digital uplink – the 'digital solution', and that is to multiplex two or more programme paths (or 'streams') in the digital domain by cascading a number of digital compression encoders together to provide a single digital data stream to the uplink chain.

This is called MCPC. In a DSNG system, there are numerous permutations possible by using a combination of both of these methods, such that you could have two RF chains, each fed by a number of digital compression coders.

Hybrid SNG/ENG trucks

Of course, some broadcasters try to have the best of both worlds – with the use of combined trucks. These are vehicles that have both a satellite uplink and a terrestrial microwave link, and are called either hybrid or 'dual purpose' ENG trucks.

The advantages of this approach are clear – you can either use the satellite uplink where you cannot get a clear microwave path out, or save on the satellite cost and use terrestrial microwave where it is possible. There is an added bonus in locations where you can achieve both a satellite link and a terrestrial microwave link – you can either feed two separate programme feeds out on each path, or achieve diversity and protection by feeding an important programme out in both directions, hence protecting it against failure on either route.

There is a particular attraction if there is a digital COFDM terrestrial microwave link being used. Whether the programme signal is going via satellite or terrestrial microwave, the signal has to be coded as an MPEG-2 signal. This means that there are savings in the amount of equipment required.

On the other hand, if it is a fully digital DSNG uplink with an analogue terrestrial microwave link, the disadvantage is that the pictures will need to be converted back to analogue before they can be transmitted over the terrestrial link. This does not save any equipment.

Hybrid SNG/ENG microwave truck (© Wolf Coach Inc.)

SNG operations – locating the uplink

The satellite uplink plainly has to be located where the story is, and the logistical and safety considerations involved as part of the decision of where to place the uplink are covered later. Hopefully it has become clear from our earlier discussions that both satellite uplinks and downlinks have to be accurately positioned and pointed at the satellite. For SNG uplinks, essentially transient in terms of their location, this is an important consideration in deciding where an uplink can be placed.

Rigging the uplink (Photo courtesy of Paul Szelers)

The uplink has to be stable, and therefore whether mounted on a vehicle or as flyaway, sitting on ground or a building roof, it must not be in a position where it could be knocked or blown off alignment.

Having found a stable position, the uplink has to be sited where it has a 'look-angle' that gives it a clear 'get-away' to the satellite. This means that it has to be sited so that there are no obstructions such as buildings, trees or passing high-sided vehicles that can block the transmission path to the satellite. In urban areas in particular, this can be quite difficult, as even a roof-mounted antenna on a truck can be obscured by a moderately tall building close by. It is of particular concern where the uplink may be located on streets running on an East–West parallel which may obstruct the path to a satellite to the North or South (depending on the hemisphere). If the satellite is on a particular low elevation angle (typically below 20°) this will increase difficulties in built-up areas.

Because of the range of types of uplinks available – both trucks and flyaways – it is not possible to give detailed instructions on how to set up and operate an uplink, and the uplink operator must rely on manufacturers' training courses and instruction manuals.

One thing to note in particular with flyaway 'rigs' – they are rarely neat and tidy and cables run everywhere like a tangle of spaghetti. Rigging often takes place under time pressure, and there is rarely time to consider in very much depth the neatest way of doing things – rigs tend to grow from the middle out.

But the following gives a general explanation of the most difficult part of the operation – finding the bird (satellite)!

Finding your satellite

When you are aligning a satellite uplink you cannot just spray signals around as you search for the satellite – this is the fundamental difference between aligning satellite links and terrestrial satellite links. Before beginning to set up the uplink, the operator should have a table of the satellites that can be 'seen' from the location. This list must include the azimuth and elevation figures for each of the satellites, and particularly important is having the magnetic azimuth figures for the satellites so that the antenna can be accurately pointed using a compass and a clinometer (a device for measuring the elevation angle). Knowing the range of satellites to the east and west of the desired satellite will assist in determining which satellite you are pointing at.

Also useful is an up-to-date copy of a satellite channel listings magazine so that any DTH satellites can be clearly identified from the programmes they are carrying, assuming of course that you have a suitable satellite receiver. Another very useful source of information of traffic on specific satellites is LyngSat at www.lyngsat.com.

Whether the uplink is truck mounted or a flyaway, the uplink needs to be placed in a level position, or if not exactly level, the amount in degrees of elevation that the uplink is displaced needs to be known – this can then be added or subtracted from the absolute elevation position required.

The feedhorn of the antenna is also connected to the satellite receiver, via a device called a LNB (low noise block downconverter), so that the uplink operator is able to view signals received from the satellite. The LNB is fitted on the end of the feed arm, very close to the feedhorn, and amplifies the very weak signal from the satellite, and frequency shifts it down from Ku- (or C-) band to what is called L-band (950–2150 MHz), which is what is required at the input to the satellite receiver.

Next you need a spectrum analyser – an instrument with the ability to repeatedly and automatically tune across a band of electromagnetic spectrum, showing the amplitude of signals present on a display screen – which covers the L-band.

Connect the spectrum analyser to the output of the LNB, and ensuring the antenna is set to the appropriate polarization (horizontal or vertical), look for the desired satellite. You can start by pointing the antenna to the azimuth and elevation angle predicted for the satellite, and then make minute adjustments in elevation and azimuth to find the satellite.

Alternatively, you can use the 'reference satellite' method. You can look for a DTH satellite (which transmits very strong signals), and then using a prediction table as shown below, calculate the differential in terms of azimuth and elevation to find the satellite you want. For example, in Northern Europe, the digital Astra DTH satellites at 28.2° East (there are several co-located in the same orbital slot) are a very clear and easy to find 'marker'. You can then find the satellite you want by calculating the differential figures from the DTH satellite and adjusting the antenna accordingly.

As an example, for the location in Aberdeen shown on the satellite listing, let us say we want to align the uplink for a transmission on Telecom 2B.

Site: Aberdeen

Satellite	Name	Azimuth (magnetic)	Elevation angle	Longitude position
Desired	Telecom 2C	178.8°	24.9°	3.00°E
DTH	Astra 2B	150.0°	19.8°	28.20°E
Differential		28.3°	5.1°	
Adjustment to find desired		Move antenna to the West by 28.3°	Increase antenna elevation by 5.1°	

To see the transmissions on Astra 2B, the LNB will need to cover the frequency range of 12.25–12.75 GHz (they are available for different receive frequency bands) – this will also enable transmissions on Telecom 2C to be seen. Using a spectrum analyser that operates over the L-band, set the controls as follows:

(1) Set the centre frequency to the equivalent local oscillator (LO) frequency of the LNB for 12.5 GHz. Supposing the LNB has a LO frequency of 11.30 GHz, then the centre frequency should be set to 12.5 GHz – 11.3 GHz = 1.2 GHz (1200 MHz).

(2) Set the span (i.e. the frequency swept across the display) to 750 MHz (i.e. 375 MHz either side of 12.5 GHz).

(3) Set the amplitude reference level to around −40 dB. This would be a typical output from an LNB receiving signals from a DTH satellite.

(4) If you now align the antenna to Astra 2C, you should see a spectrum analyser display similar to that shown in the diagram overleaf.

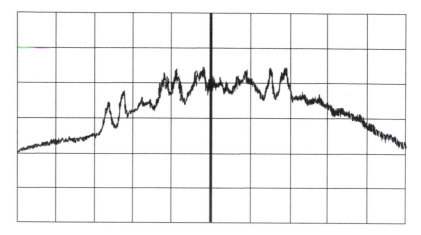

Typical spectrum analyser display from a satellite

Having found the 'reference' satellite, you can now realign the antenna to the desired satellite, and if all is well, you will be able to find it relatively easily. You will need to make iterative adjustments to the azimuth, elevation and polarization to correctly align the antenna.

Finally, you should call the satellite operator's control centre, and double check that the satellite signal carriers you can see at various frequencies confirm with what the satellite operator is radiating from the satellite.

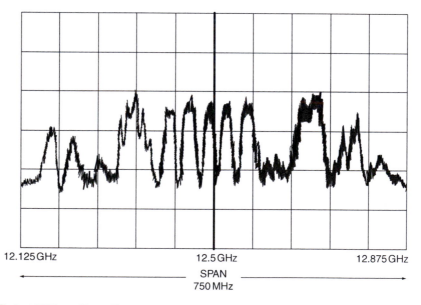

12.125 GHz   12.5 GHz   12.875 GHz

SPAN
750 MHz

Typical DTH satellite traffic spectrum analyser display

If you cannot find it, then it may be for one or more of the following reasons:

- You have misread the compass and/or inclinometer, and are looking at the wrong part of the sky
- You have miscalculated its position if using the reference satellite method
- the LNB is not the correct one for the band you are seeking
- the LNB is faulty or not working
- the information you are using is out-of-date.

Satellites also typically transmit a beacon signal, but these are usually such small signals that the typical SNG antenna is too small to receive them. Of much more use is if the satellite operator control can switch on a small pure carrier signal (i.e. no modulation) so that the uplink operator can have the spectrum analyser lined up to identify on the centre frequency of the analyser – the carrier should then pop up right in the middle of the spectrum analyser screen, and the uplink operator can then adjust the polarization of the SNG antenna to optimize this signal.

So to summarize, to set up an uplink, the operator needs the following equipment in addition to the actual uplink transmission equipment:

- compass
- clinometer
- satellite position table
- spectrum analyser
- satellite programme listings
- satellite receiver and picture monitor

SNG operations – locating the uplink

Co-ordination and line-up procedures

Each time an uplink is to undertake a transmission, there is always co-ordination via a co-ordination telephone line – which can be a land-line, cellular or satellite phone. Co-ordination is the process by which the line-up, start of transmission and end of transmission are discussed and agreed by telephone between the two points – uplink and downlink.

This will occur either between the uplink and the final destination of the transmission (such as the destination downlink control centre as usually occurs with long-term leases and some short-term leases) or between the uplink and the satellite operator's control centre (for occasional transmissions).

The satellite operator's control centre is usually in its home country, and booking information is checked and confirmed, as well as the technical parameters. If there are any problems at either point during the transmission, this is dealt with via the co-ordination line.

The number of the co-ordination line must be known to the control centre, and must be kept clear of other calls during the transmission in case of a problem that the control centre needs to alert the uplink operator about.

'Line-up' is the term used for the initial establishment of the signal from the uplink, and it is the period during which the signal is checked for technical compliance by the reception point. Normally no longer than 5 min, line-up is terminated by the commencement of the transmission. When the transmission is terminated, the end time (known as the 'goodnight') is agreed by the uplink and the satellite operator's control centre. This is particularly important for occasional transmissions where the chargeable period has to be accurately agreed and recorded for billing purposes.

Once the uplink is rigged and aligned to the correct satellite (commonly referred to as being 'panned-up'), a typical sequence for an occasional booking is as follows (the time of the start of transmission is often referred to as Z):

- Z – 10 min: Uplink calls control centre. Identifying its uplink registration, the booking details are confirmed, including uplink frequency and polarization.
- Z – 5: Line-up usually begins. With clearance from control centre, the uplink starts to transmit (brings up) an unmodulated (clean) carrier of 5 to 10% of full nominal power. The control centre checks the carrier is at the correct frequency, polarization, and nominal power with no 'out-of-band' rogue transmission – which would indicate a problem with the RF part of the uplink transmission equipment.
- Z – 3: With the carrier still at less than 10% full power, the control centre instructs modulation to be switched on – which will simply be typical modulation as the control centre may not be able to decode the digital modulation (if there is a CA on the signal). Once control centre agrees the modulated signal looks correct, power is raised to full nominal power. Control centre finally checks the signal, and agrees transmission can commence.

Lining up with the control centre (Photo courtesy of Simon Atkinson)

- Z: Chargeable period commences. Test signal is removed, and programme signal now switched to transmission.
- Z+n: End of transmission. Uplink brings down signal, and agrees the transmission end time (the goodnight) with control centre.

Over-runs

During the transmission, the uplink operator may need to extend the booking; for instance, if the 'live' slot has been moved in the news programme running order, or the tape has arrived at the last minute and there is more material to be fed than had been anticipated. A last-minute booking extension is termed an 'over-run'. Although it will be in the satellite operator's interest to grant an over-run (as it is increased income), it may not be possible if there is another booking on the same channel immediately after the booked time. Obtaining an over-run may not be possible if the uplink is unable to contact the satellite operator's control centre before the end of the booked time – the control centres can be quite busy and not always able to answer all phone calls. However, it is strictly forbidden by all satellite operators for any uplink to continue to transmit beyond the end of the booked time unless prior authorization has been obtained.

Automation

Automation has entered the broadcast process in all areas to varying degrees, and SNG is no exception. This may sound a little odd, considering the unpredictable way in which SNG systems are set up and used – after all, it is not like automating a process in a broadcast centre. But in these days of constant downward pressure of costs, combined with the element of multi-skilling that has increased in many areas, there is a natural attraction towards the use of automated processes if it saves money.

So some automation is possible, and there are two principal types of process which can be automated – acquisition of the satellite and remote operation of the system.

Automated acquisition of the satellite

The most difficult task in the operation of any SNG system, which by its very nature is never in one place for very long, is acquiring the bird. The satellite can be an elusive object to identify at times for even the most experienced operators, but the process can, surprisingly, be relatively easily automated for most operations which are based on a vehicle.

A satellite occupies a position in space that is defined by two parameters in relation to a particular location – its azimuth and elevation. By the co-ordinated usage of two devices, an automated system can be devised to find a satellite. It has to be said that this type of automated system is only suited for a vehicle-mounted rather than a flyaway system.

The two devices are a GPS unit, and a flux-gate compass. They are used in conjunction with a microprocessor control system that has satellite orbital positions programmed. This control system can then drive the antenna to the correct azimuth and elevation for the required satellite.

GPS

The Global Positioning System (GPS) was developed in the 1970s by the US Department of Defense to provide highly accurate location data, and using a constant stream of timing information generated from a highly accurate atomic clock on each satellite, GPS receivers fitted with clocks read this information. By comparing the signal from each satellite with the time in its own clock, the GPS receiver calculates the distance to each satellite and adjusts its own clock, then uses triangulation techniques to calculate its location, providing positional information accurate to less than one metre for military use. It is the technology behind the ability to provide the military with the exact positional information required for modern warfare, including the precise information required by 'smart' bombs and missiles.

The service is available to be used by commercial manufacturers of GPS equipment, albeit at a 'degraded' quality that still allows positioning to be accurate to less than 10 m. The satellites send out signals which a GPS receiver can lock onto and determine its position. The GPS unit needs to receive signals from at least three different satellites in the system to be able to accurately determine its position, and a signal from a fourth to determine its altitude. These receivers are available in many countries at very economical prices (under 200 US dollars).

GPS technology is widely used for all forms of navigation. It is also used in automated satellite acquisition systems to provide the longitude and latitude information to determine the look angle of the required satellite for antenna positioning.

The flux-gate compass is a very accurate electromagnetic compass which provides an accurate bearing (heading), and this is referenced to a nominal reference direction – usually the direction the vehicle is pointing or the antenna is normally sitting at after deployment.

Automation in operation

On arriving at site, the vehicle can be readied for transmission. The required satellite is selected from a menu list on the control panel, and the GPS unit and the flux-gate compass feed the positional information of the uplink to the antenna control system. From this information, the control system can calculate the required antenna azimuth and elevation for the selected satellite.

Under control of the automated acquisition system, which is activated by a single button press, the antenna is raised from its lowered (park) position to a predetermined nominal elevation. It then rotates to the satellite's azimuth, and elevates to the calculated elevation angle.

Some systems go one step further in sophistication, and use a known strong signal from the satellite to determine the correcting pointing angle by calculating the offset in azimuth and elevation from this known signal. The antenna controller, having used the GPs and flux-gate compass to aim the motorized antenna, then uses a control voltage derived from this known 'beacon' signal to 'auto peak' the antenna. On finding the 'beacon' signal, the control system fine tunes the antenna in azimuth and elevation (by jogging it left, right, up and down) to optimise the signal level from the beacon, ensuring that the antenna is accurately pointed.

Advantages and disadvantages of automation

Such a system has the undeniable advantage that technology can replace the highly tuned skills of a good uplink operator in finding the satellite. Staff with lesser technical skills are just as able to press the button to set the system in motion. This, combined with other technical functions that could be automated or pre-programmed in the operation of an uplink, could very well allow the use of journalists or any other spare pair of hands to operate the uplink – though the style of operation may be subject to a satellite operator restriction.

However, one must consider that the typical SNG system is an already sophisticated set of equipment, and the addition of an automated system for finding the satellite is 'just another thing to go wrong'. If the system fails to find the satellite, it could be anyone of a number of processes that have failed. If such a system is used by an experienced uplink operator to save time, then if it fails, the satellite can still be found by manual methods, and the antenna correctly aligned. But in the hands of an unskilled operator, the transmission will be lost.

Its use is perhaps best seen on a small journalist-operated vehicle, which has a relatively simple function and usage.

Fully remote operation

This is an extension of the automated acquisition system, to a level where the entire uplink is remotely controlled. It has been implemented both on vehicles and on some flyaway systems, where remote control can be used once the antenna has been aligned manually with some additional 'pointing aids' for the non-technical operator.

The remote control package allows control of all the key operational parameters by a separate communications channel. This channel can be provided by a plain old telephone service (POTS), an Inmarsat satphone, or even a separate satellite channel that is activated via the antenna once it is correctly aligned.

The level of control can be relatively sophisticated, but as a basic minimum it will control the digital encoder, modulator and HPA.

However, as with the automatic acquisition systems, a failure of the system can be due to any number of reasons, and therefore there is a compromise that has to be accepted if opting for this mode of operation. Not many news organizations would want to deploy such a system in the hands of a non-technical operator on a 'big story', and if the use of such a system is going to be constrained by the type of story it can be used on, it can be argued that it is a false economy.

It may seem here that we are debating whether someone whose primary job is not a technical one – e.g. a journalist – is capable of operating an SNG uplink with the different automated controls described. That is not the issue – it is more whether if, for example, a journalist is trying to do other jobs as well as their own, something will suffer. Newsgathering is not a serial process, i.e. jobs and tasks that have to be done do not concatenate neatly together. There are task overlaps on the timeline of reporting a story, and some even run directly in parallel. At times, it is not 'a matter of many hands make light work', but that many hands make it happen – on air and on time. On most stories, the journalist is busy simply keeping up with the story. On rapidly breaking events the requirement to repeatedly go 'live' for a string of different outlets can mean that the journalist is no longer effectively reporting the story as it carries on developing and unfolding, as they are still stuck in front of the camera reporting what has become 'old' news.

Inmarsat and the use of videophones

In the last year or so, everyone has seen widespread use of the 'Videophone' – the latest newsgathering tool that has become the ubiquitous tool for front-line newsgathering. No discussion of current SNG techniques can overlook the videophone phenomenon.

We will look at how the videophone works in a minute, but first, we need to look at the means of transmission that the videophone use – the Inmarsat satellite telephone system. The Inmarsat system is also used to send high quality pictures – albeit not in real time – using a system called Store and Forward.

Inmarsat system

Originally designed for maritime communication, the Inmarsat system has now expanded to other market sectors, including newsgathering. In recent years, the Inmarsat system has become a vital tool for global newsgathering, used not only for person-to-person voice communication for 'keeping-in-touch', but for transmitting back various types of media – high-quality still pictures, studio-quality audio for radio reports, and even TV pictures 'live' using ruggedized videophone units, or non-real time transfer using Store and Forward video units.

Using Inmarsat satphones, pictures and sound can be sent from almost anywhere on the globe. This versatility, combined with increasingly compact equipment, has enabled Inmarsat to become a significant force in news-gathering.

The Inmarsat system consists of four geostationary satellites operating in L-band (see page 85) that cover most of the Earth's surface and have a range of services with different capabilities. There is a satellite above each of the ocean regions – Indian, Pacific and Atlantic (there are actually two over the Atlantic). Between them, the main (global) beams of the satellites provide overlapping coverage of the whole surface of the Earth apart from the poles (see map opposite).

A call from an Inmarsat mobile terminal goes directly to the satellite overhead, which routes it back down to a 'gateway' station on the ground called a land earth station (LES). From there, the call is passed into the public phone network.

All services offer the same common core feature – instant and on-demand dial-up access limited only by satellite capacity and coverage using portable mobile terminals. Those used on land (as opposed to maritime or aero units) are referred to as land mobile earth stations (LMES). Typically the LMES offer two types of service – voice and data. Voice speaks for itself(!), and data generally comes in two flavours – low speed 9.6 kbps typically for use with a laptop, and high speed data (HSD) which runs at 64 kbps – the same speed as ISDN lines in offices and homes.

Because of our interest in newsgathering, we will use the term for the LMES used by all newsgatherers – the satellite telephone or more often referred to as the 'satphone'.

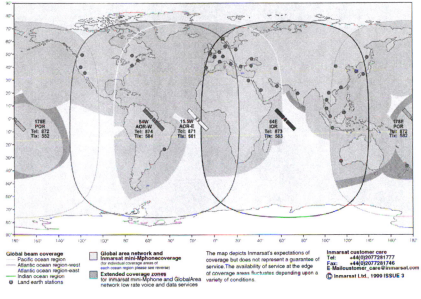

| 178E
POR
Tel: 872
Tlx: 582 | | 54W
AOR-W
Tel: 874
Tlx: 584 | 15.5W
AOR-E
Tel: 871
Tlx: 581 | | 64E
IOR
Tel: 873
Tlx: 583 | | 178E
POR
Tel: 872
Tlx: 582 |

Global beam coverage
- Pacific ocean region
- Atlantic ocean region-west
- Atlantic ocean region-east
- Indian ocean region
- Land earth stations

Global area network and Inmarsat mini-Mphonecoverage
(for individual coverage areas of each ocean region please see reverse)

Extended coverage zones
for Inmarsat mini-Mphone and GlobalArea network low rate voice and data services

The map depicts Inmarsat's expectations of coverage but does not represent a guarantee of service.The availability of service at the edge of coverage areas fluctuates depending upon a variety of conditions.

Inmarsat customer care
Tel: +44(0)2077281777
Fax: +44(0)2077281746
E Mail:customer_care@inmarsat.com
© Inmarsat Ltd., 1999 ISSUE 3

Inmarsat coverage map (© Inmarsat Ltd)

The various types of satphone

There is a whole family of satphones of various types for various applications. But we are going to focus only on two – Inmarsat Mini-M and Inmarsat GAN – as these are the ones used widely for newsgathering. Both of these types of phones are compact, light (and easy to carry), and simple to operate.

Inmarsat Mini-M

The Mini-M satphone was introduced in 1996 and is approximately the size of a notebook computer. The satphone has the option of using a SIM card so that service is bought and access-controlled in the same way as GSM. The available services are voice, data and fax, but with no HSD service. From the point of view of keeping in touch in hazardous areas, the Mini-M satphone has a distinct advantage for newsgatherers. It is available in vehicle-mounted versions from a few manufacturers, and this allows a small and relatively discreet auto-tracking antenna to be easily fitted to the roof of a car, with the handset and control unit inside the car. This has a great advantage in that the satphone is permanently rigged, and calls can therefore be made or received on the move, rather than having to stop and get out of a vehicle to set the satphone up before use.

Inmarsat and the use of videophones

141

Inmarsat Mini-M satphone (© Nera Satellite Services Ltd)

Inmarsat GAN

Inmarsat GAN is the most common type of satphone used by newsgatherers for not only keeping in touch but also for sending back reports. Sometimes referred to as Inmarsat 'M4' satphones (this was the project name during the GAN system development), the terminals are the size of a laptop computer, weighing under 4 kg (10 lb), and offer voice, fax, file transfer and HSD at up to 64 kbps. The coverage of Inmarsat GAN is, like Mini-M, mostly limited to continental land masses only. The Inmarsat GAN satphone is shown in the figure opposite.

Although technically it is possible to use Inmarsat satphones in virtually any country in the world, some countries either do not permit its use, or if they do, make it prohibitively expensive to do so. Inmarsat is encouraging those countries to remove or reduce the regulatory barriers that restrict or prevent the use of its equipment within their borders.

Some countries prohibit any use of mobile satellite communications equipment, while others permit it only in particular circumstances, such as for disaster relief or emergencies, or in limited geographical areas.

Anyone considering taking an Inmarsat satphone to another country is advised to contact the authorities in the country they plan to visit, to get up-to-date information on any conditions attached to use of the terminal in the visited country. Failure to secure the appropriate approvals is likely at the very least to result in confiscation of the equipment at the point of entry to the country, or even in some countries, arrest on the grounds of suspected espionage.

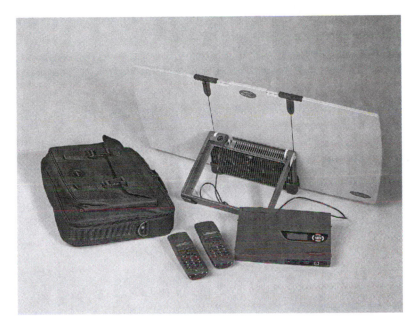

Inmarsat GAN satphone (© Nera Satcom AS)

The dramatic impact on newsgathering of using Inmarsat GAN satphones is the ability to transmit news pictures from places where:

- there is no infrastructure for TV transmissions
- local politics or the overall logistics prevents the deployment of conventional SNG flyaways
- the news story has not developed to the point where it is considered cost-effective to deploy an SNG flyaway.

The GAN phone is designed to work with Integrated Services Digital Network (ISDN) services, used for public dial-up data service in many countries around the world.

As the ISDN numbering system follows the same pattern as the normal telephone system, dialling is carried out in exactly the same manner as making a normal telephone call. The subscriber number is used with the same area codes as the telephone network and international codes are also the same and used in the same way as for the telephone network.

Calls to an Inmarsat GAN satphone are made in exactly the same manner as a normal international call. Dial the home country's international access code, followed by the Ocean Region code and finally the number of the satphone. The Ocean Region Codes are:

Atlantic Ocean Region – East   871
Pacific Ocean Region   872

143

| Indian Ocean Region | 873 |
| Atlantic Ocean Region – West | 874 |

For dialling from a satphone to a landline, the following parameters on the Inmarsat GAN satphone need to be set prior to dialling the destination ISDN number:

- the LES (the earth station gateway) to be used
- set satphone in HSD mode

The procedures for checking and setting these parameters are given in the satphone manufacturers operating guide.

Video-conferencing and videophones

Video-conferencing is the technique for enabling two-way video, audio and data signals, at relatively low quality, to be used for live interaction over a communications circuit. Video-conferencing is used either on a one-to-one basis, or by groups of people who gather in a specific setting (often a conference room) to communicate with others. As mentioned earlier, we have seen the development of ruggedized video-conferencing units designed for newsgathering to be used in the field – the videophone.

Videophones

The videophone is essentially a video-conferencing unit adapted for field use. Certainly, the quality of transmission cannot match normal SNG equipment, but the videophone's key advantage is that it is relatively easy to set up and tote around. The videophone unit used by many TV reporters weighs less than 5 kg and connects to a camera and one or two Inmarsat GAN satphones for live transmission of pictures. The whole system is carried in five laptop-size bags, can take an experienced operator less than 10 min to set up, and be powered via a car's cigarette lighter.

In the Iraq conflict in 2003, we saw widespread use of videophones by 'embedded' reporters working with front-line military units. But a particular incident in the Afghan conflict a few years earlier clearly illustrates the advantages and power of the videophone.

In November 2001 during the Afghanistan conflict, CNN correspondent Nic Robertson crossed into Taliban-controlled territory and within minutes was reporting live on the air, bringing news to the world from Afghanistan. After gathering the news on the ground and interviewing a Taliban military commander, he did not want to wait. Because the Taliban had set up strict reporting restrictions, the CNN crew smuggled videophones past border guards, enabling them immediately to broadcast footage from their hotel balcony against the backdrop of Kabul. Although images from the videophone are of lower quality than those from 'conventional' SNG uplinks, the videophone allowed CNN to broadcast scenes of the war almost half an hour earlier than rival broadcasters who drove to an SNG uplink facility to send their reports.

While the images are not of true broadcast quality, videophones have become popular with journalists travelling light. The videophone first became famous in April 2001, when CNN used it to broadcast exclusive live footage of a US spy plane crew leaving Hainan Island in China after having been held hostage.

They may not have been the world's greatest pictures, but they were live. The images were jerky because the reporter pointed the camera at the runway to capture the plane's tyres leaving the ground. Often called the Talking Head (named after the pioneering manufacturer's model), the videophone was designed to provide live pictures of a correspondent's moving head on a straight PTC mid-shot, not varying and moving TV footage.

145

The system typically consists of two units – the ruggedized field unit (the videophone) and a studio unit. The system can actually send video and audio in both directions at the same time, so a reporter cannot only hear the studio but he/she can also see the studio output too. The system can either use one ISDN circuit to operate at 64 kbps, or by making two calls, operate at 128 kbps so giving higher quality. The higher data rate allows the system to cope with more movement in the picture, or if desired improve the audio quality to studio standard (48 kbps rather than 16 kbps) in lieu of a smaller improvement in the picture quality.

So how is this equipment set up? At the receive end in the studio, you need an ISDN line and the studio transceiver. In the field you need one of the following combinations:

- A single Inmarsat GAN satphone which provides an ISDN interface but is only capable of single channel operation so you can only connect at 64 kbps.
- Any two Inmarsat GAN satphones each of which can provide 64 kbps and a videophone which split the two channels of a 128 kbps ISDN-2 call across two single channel ISDN connections, i.e. two satphones.

At least one satphone manufacturer makes a dual channel GAN (although it is very bulky) and another has an interconnecting cable between the two satphones – in both cases a videophone can make 128 kbps calls.

As we know, TV operates at 25 or 30 fps, and video-conferencing that operates at a true speed of 15 fps or greater looks acceptable for most users. If operating at rates as low as 10 fps, picture jitter is noticeable, and a person speaking will show an apparent lack of continuity.

The videophone will, once the call is connected, typically take 5–10 s for each end of the link to synchronize and connect.

Videophone in use (© 7E Communications Ltd)

Store and Forward

An alternative to the use of the low quality videophone is a Store and Forward system. It is important to note immediately that such systems do not operate in 'live' mode – they are intended for the transmission of material at higher quality, slower than real time. This means that every minute of material recorded will actually take several minutes to send.

A 'live' video transmission of a quality generally acceptable for a news broadcast requires a connection with a capacity of at least 2 Mbps. Clearly nothing near this data rate is currently available with the Inmarsat GAN service and to achieve this in a remote location, away from fixed high capacity terrestrial circuits, normally requires the use of a full-blown SNG system. However, although the Inmarsat GAN service is commonly used for live videophone broadcasts, a data rate of 64 or 128 kbps is simply not capable of providing sufficient capacity for high quality video.

However, by encoding the high quality video in a process where it is digitized and compressed at high bit rate, and then stored on a computer hard disk, the data can then be later transmitted through the Inmarsat GAN HSD system. Once received at the studio, it can then be integrated into the news broadcast for transmission.

This process is called 'Store and Forward' and gives users the ability to transmit high quality video and audio at relatively low data rates. Although the material is not live, it need not be more than a few hours old and the tradeoff in terms of portability makes it a very attractive alternative. In addition, Inmarsat GAN HSD channels are assigned on-demand and more conveniently available over a much wider area of the globe than Ku- or C-band SNG capacity.

The fundamental principle of the system is that video is played into a Store and Forward unit, which digitizes the video and stores it as a data file on the hard disk of a PC. Once this process has been completed, the Store and Forward unit can be connected to an Inmarsat GAN satphone, and a HSD call established to a companion unit at the destination. When the connection has been established the video/audio data file is transferred over the link and recorded as a data file at the destination. On completion of the transfer, the data file is played out as converted real-time video and audio.

As with the videophone, by using two satphones, the data rate is doubled, and for Store and Forward the file transmission time is halved.

The key to successful implementation of Store and Forward techniques is in the coding (digitization and compression) of the video. Uncompressed digital video would create enormous data files of gigabyte proportions. However, compression of the video during encoding reduces the file size to much more manageable proportions. In fact, compression ratios between 25:1 and 100:1 are typical with the actual compression selection depending upon the desired video quality.

Choosing a high sampling rate will result in higher quality pictures than a lower sampling rate, but will increase the transmission time. Store and Forward units offer a range of sampling rates, the highest of which will result in very good quality MPEG-2 pictures and sound being transferred at a rate of typically 50:1. One minute of video will therefore take approximately 50 min to arrive at the other end.

The length of the video and the sampling rate at which the video is digitized determine the size of the transmitted data file. The transmission times are thus fundamentally determined by three factors – the video sequence length, the video coding rate of the file and the data channel rate of 64 kbps for the Inmarsat GAN HSD service.

The video can be coded as an MPEG-2 or MPEG-4 compressed file. Some pictures coded at a lower data rate than typical MPEG-2 can have a 'filmic' look, reminiscent of 16 mm film. The quality of these pictures is often compared to VHS, but the overall effect is quite satisfactory for a news insert on a breaking story. The quality is often much improved if the shot scenes have high light levels, so that the pictures have few dark areas.

Store and Forward hardware

Highly portable Store and Forward systems were originally developed in the mid-1990s weighing only about 12 kg (25 lb) and designed for use in rugged conditions. A common system used in newsgathering in the field was the Toko VAST-p (no longer made). The VAST-p unit has been in use with a number of newsgatherers (both broadcasters and news agencies) for a number of years, but has now been superseded by newer technological solutions.

Camcorder

Inmarsat satphone

Laptop with software encoding (and editing software)

Store and Forward process

148

With the development of ever more powerful laptop PCs, there are now several Store and Forward systems that are based on software packages that run on a high-end laptop. The current generation of Store and Forward technology is based on using a laptop computer and a software encoder (unlike the earlier Toko VAST-p hardware encoding unit).

The video and audio is 'captured' as it is played into the laptop in real time via a 'Firewire' connection. The video and audio can then be edited if required using any one of a number of video editing packages of the user's choosing, depending on the facilities and price.

Once it has been captured, and edited if required, the material is then compressed by software on the laptop using a software encoder using any one of a number of compression standards – the favourites at the time of writing are DivX, MPEG-2, MPEG-4 or Windows© Media 9.

The completed compressed file can then be sent via FTP (file transfer protocol) via an Inmarsat satphone (Mini-M or GAN) to the studio for subsequent transmission. A number of manufacturers produce systems based on this type of technology.

Store and Forward

Inmarsat satphone operation

The following explanations give an idea of the differences in operation between the Inmarsat GAN and Mini-M satphones, and demonstrate how units of each type are typically assembled and operated. These are currently the two most common Inmarsat systems used by newsgatherers.

Inmarsat GAN

There is a limited selection of brands of Inmarsat GAN satphones, and the Inmarsat GAN satphone typically consists of two parts – the antenna and the transceiver unit – integrated together.

The unit has a fold out panel antenna, and the whole unit is pointed approximately towards the satellite. The unit typically has both an audible and visual display of signal strength, and as the unit is rotated slowly towards the satellite, the signal strength indication will increase. The elevation angle of the antenna also has to be adjusted to obtain optimum signal strength.

Why is the antenna-pointing not as critical as for the larger SNG uplinks? The answer lies in the operating frequency of Inmarsat satphones. They all operate in L-band (around 1600 MHz), and therefore because the beamwidth is considerably wider, less pointing accuracy is required.

Because the pointing is not so critical, it is possible to even transmit videophone pictures from the decks of large warships. Incidentally this can be done with Ku-band SNG uplinks as well, but the antenna needs to be only around 1 m, and will need manual tracking as the ship moves through a relatively calm sea.

Siting the satphone

To operate successfully, the satphone needs to be able to 'see' one of the four Inmarsat satellites. When siting the antenna, a compass is used to check that there is a clear view towards the satellite – to the south if in the Northern hemisphere, and to the north if in the Southern Hemisphere. The satphone can be used inside a building if the antenna is pointing out through a window – the window does not need to be open, but beware of metallized coatings on the glass used to prevent glare or offer privacy. The window obviously needs to offer a view of the sky in the right direction.

- Do not use the compass near the satphone while it is switched on, as the electromagnetic field from the satphone antenna can cause a false reading.
- Do not try and take a reading from the compass near vehicles (metal affects the reading), nor inside buildings, as many modern structures have an integral steel frame that will affect a compass reading. Tall buildings or trees close-by must not obstruct the view towards the satellite. For safety reasons, the antenna should not be pointed towards areas where people may pass or gather, and ensure that no cables create a trip hazard.

A few seconds after the satphone is switched on, the handset display should give various status indications, telling the user which LES is selected (usually the one last used). To make a reliable HSD call, the antenna must be pointing very accurately at the chosen Ocean Region satellite. This is not the case for simple voice calls, which with a much lower data rate do not need such critical alignment. There is usually a chart supplied with the terminal that will give an estimate of the azimuth and the elevation of the antenna. The whole satphone may be rotated until the antenna points in the direction indicated by the compass. The terminal display gives an indication of signal strength.

Safety

The antenna produces significant levels of non-ionizing radiation and the manufacturers' recommendations for minimum clear distances in front of the antenna must be followed: 2–3 m is a typical 'safe zone'. Standing behind the antenna is perfectly safe, and it is advisable to mark out the safe zone with visual warning tape. However, in HSD mode, satphones have an automatic transmission cut-out which operates within 15 s of an obstruction appearing in front of the antenna. This is not the case when it is operating in voice-only mode, when care must be taken that no one stands in front of the antenna. Such is the resilience of the data link for voice transmissions, the satphone may be able to maintain a connection even with a person standing in front of the antenna.

Operating

All commands are keyed into the DECT handset, which displays all information needed. Operational controls are accessed from the handset with error messages and the progress of the call displayed on the handset. Once aligned and set up, the satphone is ready for operation. Each manufacturer's unit will vary in the keystrokes required to set the mode of operation and dialling sequence. Different codes are used in the dialling sequence to establish the type of call (voice, HSD, etc.) as indicated earlier in this chapter. Any additional units such as videophone, digital audio encoder, or Store and Forward units will also need to be connected before an HSD call can be made.

Inmarsat Mini-M

The operation of the Inmarsat Mini-M satphone is very straightforward. The satphone comes in a small laptop-sized case, and the antenna is usually integral to the case. It is simply a matter of flipping the antenna up, pointing it approximately in the direction of the satellite, and optimizing the position in azimuth and elevation to get the strongest signal strength. Once this has been done, the handset can be used to dial the call directly. Because the RF power from the Mini-M satphones is much lower, there need only be a one metre area kept clear in front of the satphone for safety reasons.

Inmarsat satphone operation

151

Satellite regulatory issues

Regulation

Operating SNG uplinks virtually anywhere in the world requires some degree of administrative process to be undertaken, and any operation has to take place within the international prescribed limits of spectrum. These individual national administrative procedures are used to regulate SNG uplinks both in terms of political and technical controls. The constant push to provide the latest news is the driver behind allowing SNG greater freedom, particularly into places where it is not wanted and even viewed with mistrust and fear. Broadcasting and telecommunications are matters of national security and social policy in many countries, and in some countries, the concept of foreign newsgatherers bringing in their own transmitting equipment is an issue of sovereignty.

To operate an SNG uplink system anywhere in the world, there are normally three areas of administration that have to be covered:

(1) Permission has to be granted to the uplink operator, on either a temporary or permanent basis, to operate the uplink in the country and area where it is to be operated.
(2) The SNG uplink operator has to obtain authority, usually by way of registration, with satellite system operators who may be providing the space segment to be used, to access that space segment with the uplink equipment.
(3) Space segment has to be secured by way of a satellite transponder/channel booking.

To fully appreciate the administrative context within which SNG operates, we need to briefly look at the regulatory aspects of spectrum. There are a bewildering number of organizations and bodies involved in the setting of standards, regulation and administration of the spectrum. Amongst all of this, we need to understand where the process of SNG overlaps with international and national regulation.

Spectrum

There is a constant pressure for the resources of bandwidth and power by telecommunications services providers seeking to deliver data, telephony and video services, particularly in the frequency spectrum used for satellite communications. The desire to deliver more services to more people has never been greater nor technologically more feasible, and to meet this pressure there is a need to be ever more efficient in the allocation and use of spectrum.

The known electromagnetic spectrum ranges from nothing to gamma radiation, with visible light just over half way up the spectrum.

Electromagnetic spectrum can be viewed as a natural element, such as water or air, but only available in a relatively controlled amount to be useful. It

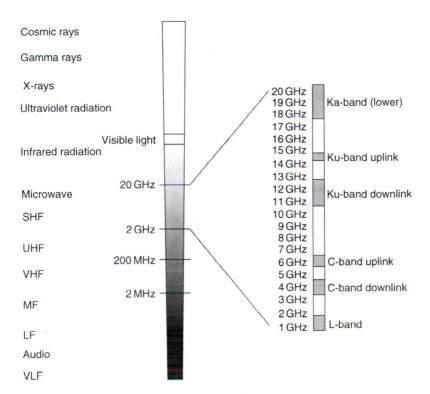

Cosmic rays

Gamma rays

X-rays

Ultraviolet radiation

Visible light

Infrared radiation

20 GHz

Microwave

SHF

2 GHz

UHF

200 MHz

VHF

2 MHz

MF

LF

Audio

VLF

20 GHz	
19 GHz	Ka-band (lower)
18 GHz	
17 GHz	
16 GHz	
15 GHz	
14 GHz	Ku-band uplink
13 GHz	
12 GHz	Ku-band downlink
11 GHz	
10 GHz	
9 GHz	
8 GHz	
7 GHz	
6 GHz	C-band uplink
5 GHz	
4 GHz	C-band downlink
3 GHz	
2 GHz	
1 GHz	L-band

Commercial satellite frequency bands of interest for SNG are shown expanded

can be imagined that without international agreement and regulation of usage there would be chaos. Each country could use whatever spectrum and transmitter power level they pleased, but as a natural resource and no respecter of man's political boundaries, the airwaves would be crowded with transmissions interfering with each other. Anyone who has tried to listen to short-wave or medium-wave radio at night will hear this type of interference as atmospheric conditions alter at night to 'throw' the signals further afield. There is also a significant amount of interference from space affecting many parts of the frequency spectrum.

The international regulation of the spectrum in fact deals with 'normal' conditions, and cannot fully take account of random atmospheric effects caused by the onset of night or abnormal weather conditions, which can particularly affect the lower end of the spectrum as used for most radio transmissions.

There are a number of regional and global standards-setting organizations, which are linked either directly or voluntarily. There is, however, a single global body that oversees all aspects of the use of spectrum – the ITU – which encompasses all administration of spectrum.

Satellite regulatory issues

ITU (International Telecommunications Union)

The ITU is concerned with international co-operation in the use of telecommunications and the RF spectrum, and with promoting and facilitating the development, expansion and operation of telecommunications networks in developing countries. It is the leading world body for the co-ordination and development of technical and operating standards for telecommunications and radiocommunications (including satellite) services.

The ITU is an intergovernmental organization (IGO), within which public and private sectors co-operate for the development of all telecommunications for the common good. It creates and defines through agreement international regulations and treaties governing all terrestrial and space uses of the frequency spectrum as well as the use of the geostationary satellite orbit. Within this framework, countries adopt their national telecommunications legislation. However, it is important to realize that the ITU does not have the power to impose regulations – it is not a supra-national power – and its strength is through agreement between member countries.

As well as administering frequency allocations for satellite use, the ITU also acts as the global co-ordinating body for the allocation of orbital slot positions for satellites. The ITU allocates sectors of the geostationary arc nominally to countries in the region below each arc sector.

National control and trans-border issues

The movement of mobile satellite transmission equipment around the world is often fraught with difficulties. Some countries prohibit any use of mobile satellite communications equipment totally, while others permit it only in particular circumstances, such as for disaster relief or emergencies, or in limited geographical areas. High licence fees, taxes and Customs duties cause significant difficulties for newsgatherers; in some countries additional 'type-approval' is sometimes demanded, even though the equipment has been type-approved elsewhere or meets internationally recognized standards, as a further hindrance.

Often these regulatory barriers exist because the country does not have a policy or regulatory framework covering mobile satellite telecommunications or because they fear 'bypass' of their terrestrial network (even in regions where there is no network to bypass) which will reduce their telecommunications revenues.

The control of SNG

The National Administrations dealing with telecommunications, even in these days of increasing privatization, are still in general under government direction, and they control access to satellite capacity by SNG uplinks to varying degrees. The level of control varies from countries where the use of SNG uplinks cannot even be contemplated, to countries where there is a highly regulated control system for allowing access to space segment by SNG uplinks through licensing and frequency clearance. The latter is often used as a way of generating a lucrative income stream.

Cross-border issues are probably the largest remaining problem in the free movement of SNG. Newsgatherers always want to take their own facilities into a foreign country if at all feasible.

The technology allowing easy movement of SNG uplinks has advanced at a far more rapid rate than political and regulatory recognition in a significant number of countries. Although many National Administrations allow SNG within their borders operated by their own nationals, many still forbid foreign operators from entering their country.

National controls

There are two main reasons for reluctance by national governments to allow free movement of SNG uplinks across national borders.

First, there is the fear of the power of unbounded dissemination of information that the use of SNG can bring, and many countries have been very slow to react to the rapid changes in technology.

Many governments are suspicious of the motives of newsgatherers who wish to operate uplinks, fearing open criticism of their political regimes which their own population may see or hear coming back via broadcasts from abroad. So

155

they forbid any news organizations using SNG within their borders as a matter of political control. They may not even allow their own broadcasters to use this equipment, and certainly not allow foreign newsgathering agencies to bring in their own SNG equipment.

Some allow foreign SNG uplinks to operate but insist on government supervision during transmissions, including 'screening' tapes before they can be fed. The ease with which foreign broadcasters are able to comment on policies and actions is a direct reflection of the fear of the power of the operation of an SNG uplink.

It may be that a government has no legislation to cope with licensing the use of SNG uplinks, though this is increasingly changing in many countries. Governments may allow the use of SNG by their own national entities, either a single monopoly supplier, or a limited and controlled number of providers. A licence or access fee may be levied if SNG equipment is to be allowed into a country. Some foreign newsgatherers may pay this simply to obtain the flexibility that having their own facility can give them, or they may decide not to bring in their own uplinks and use the facilities available within the country.

In general, there are two levels or types of access granted to SNG uplink operators, depending on the degree of advancement of telecommunication administration in a country. These categories are loosely permissions and licences. The point at which a permission can be termed a licence is a little blurred. There is a further control, called frequency co-ordination, which is related to purely technical considerations of potential interference by the SNG uplink.

Incidentally, it is often the case that where a permission has to be obtained with a national administration which is apprehensive or obstructive to the idea of a foreign operator sending in their own uplink, local contact on the ground is by far the best way of moving matters forward. This is often a cultural issue, where the 'western' practice of making demands by telephone or fax is seen as being insulting, and 'pressing the flesh' over cups of iced tea or coffee is far more likely to produce results. Financial inducements to officials are common in many cultures and do not hold the same negative connotation as in western culture.

Licences

The approximate differentiation between permissions and licences is the legislative structure underpinning telecommunications that exists within a country. In countries with a statutory system regulating the use of telecommunications, including SNG, a structure of licence issue is usually in place, subject to certain provisions or restrictions. Licences can be granted on a 'per occasion' basis or even on an annual or regularly renewable basis. Typically SNG uplink operators in their native country are granted permission to operate under the terms of a licence.

Obtaining a licence may involve a number of steps. It may involve simply filling out a form giving details of the technical parameters of the uplink. It may require details of any satellite system registrations the uplink already has, or a declaration as to whether it is going to be connected to a telecommunications network, or operate as a stand-alone uplink – which is typically the case for SNG. It may involve also submitting what are referred to as 'range patterns'. These are frequency test patterns of the performance of the antenna measured on a test range, and define the performance of the antenna, and in particular prove its 'sidelobe' performance i.e. its directional performance. This is particularly important as it shows the integrity of the antenna, particularly demonstrating that it will not cause interference.

Upon approval of the technical parameters, and payment of the necessary fee, the licence is issued for the specified period. There may be a further fee for renewal or if alteration to the licence is required due to changed parameters of the uplink system.

Some countries do not require so much technical information, or proof that the antenna meets a particular standard. They simply require the uplink to be registered with them, and the requisite fees to be paid.

In the United Kingdom, licences are granted on a per occasion basis, or on an annual basis, by the Radiocommunications Agency (RA). Fees are typically £1000 per annum, for a digital TES (transportable earth station – an acronym we saw earlier for an SNG uplink).

Frequency clearance

In some countries, frequency clearance is required for each individual transmission of the SNG uplink – this is in addition to having a licence, and the licence may be withdrawn if it is discovered that frequency clearance has not been obtained. The purpose of the frequency clearance is normally to ensure that the uplink transmissions will not interfere with any other transmission. The most likely services that can be interfered with are terrestrial point-to-point microwave links operating at or near the same frequency, where the transmission beam from the uplink may cut through or very near to the point-to-point terrestrial microwave link path.

The parameters typically required for frequency clearance are:

- the transmit frequency of the uplink
- its location
- the satellite to which it is going to work
- the orbital position of the satellite
- the ITU Emission Code
- the times and dates of the transmission(s).

The ITU Emission Code is an internationally recognized alphanumeric code that defines the transmission characteristics of the signal.

The national authorities will either send back an acknowledgement authorizing the transmission, or in some countries no reply can be interpreted as consent. Frequency clearances are compulsory in C-band in most developed countries, and may take weeks or months to obtain due to the high likelihood of interference with terrestrial point-to-point microwave links commonly operating in this band, which may require international co-ordination.

National control and trans-border issues

However in Ku-band, a frequency clearance is sometimes necessary only in the 14.25–14.50 GHz band; as this is often shared with microwave links, co-ordination is required. In the lower part of the Ku-band used for SNG uplinks (14.0–14.25 GHz), co-ordination is often not required as this is an area of the band exclusive to satellite applications in many countries.

However, many countries do not require any frequency clearance at all in the Ku-band, e.g. the United States; therefore this is one less piece of administration that the SNG uplink operator needs to be concerned about.

The 'legitimate' use of SNG uplinks involves varying degrees of processes of administration in different countries. Although these processes can be seen as irksome in the face of meeting the challenge trying to cover breaking news, or even sustaining basic news coverage, it is essential in the long term for the ordered and controlled use of a scarce natural resource.

The political control of the use of SNG uplinks is likely to remain a continuing problem, though there are signs in the easing of restrictions in a number of countries that have previously taken a rigid stance in opposing the use of such equipment. However, for almost every sovereign state, telecommunications and access to radio spectrum is almost invariably as much a political issue as a technical one.

ITU SNG handbook

To help those seeking guidance on who to approach in a country, the ITU publishes the 'SNG User's Guide Online' online (www.itu.int/ITU-R/study-groups/sng/). This provides information to assist a foreign broadcaster to bring their SNG terminal to a country (or area) and obtain a temporary operating licence.

The 'SNG User's Guide' includes:

- the service operational characteristics
- the satellite characteristics
- the interconnection capabilities with SNG terminals
- a standardized set of procedures required for the temporary authorization of SNG transmissions
- a regularly updated list of satellite system operators and service providers
- a list of designated contact points to authorize operation of SNG services in a given country (or area).

Satellite operators

Satellite operators are the companies that build, launch and operate satellites, and they are in business to make money by operating satellites to provide telecommunication services. Before they can earn a single dollar in revenue from the use of a satellite, an operator will have to spend hundreds of millions of dollars to build the satellite, launch it by rocket into orbit, and get it working. Once it is in orbit, it costs money year on year to operate a ground control facility and keep the satellite flying for around 15 years.

We will look briefly at who actually operates the satellites, describing some of the principal global and regional satellite systems, focussing on those that allow access for SNG, and how these can be accessed by SNG uplinks. It is not possible here to detail every satellite that is in orbit, for the information changes quite often – it is best to consult the satellite operators directly, many of whom publish their current fleets on their websites. It is also important to note that information for any satellite system we do give here is only current as at the time of writing, and will probably have changed by the time you read this.

Overall, there are more regional systems than global systems. Apart from carrying SNG traffic (which is a relatively minor proportion of their traffic), these systems carry services such as:

- public telephony and data, including Internet connectivity
- private data networks for businesses
- direct-to-home (DTH)/direct broadcasting services (DBS) for TV and radio
- backbone video/audio distribution services.

Many satellites are in orbit to provide only these other services and do not cater for the SNG market at all. The range of services is wide, and the demand in all these areas is growing, feeding a multi-billion dollar global industry.

It is also worth noting that some organizations both operate their own satellites and lease capacity on a long-term basis on other satellite systems as well, usually in order to provide as diverse offering of services and wide area of coverage as possible.

All satellite system operators, whatever their size, are aiming to provide as much of a 'one-stop shop' for their customers, whether it be purely regional service, or where trans-global connectivity is required. So let us look at a few of the main players.

Intelsat

We will begin with Intelsat, which was the first satellite system available for trans-global commercial use, and was also the first system that allowed international access for SNG. As the first global commercial satellite system, it still holds a commanding position in the global market, but has come under intense pressure from competition from other systems in the last 15 years. The early history of Intelsat is closely bound up with US dominance in satellite communications.

Intelsat remains the primary provider of services to developing nations and more remote areas of the globe. Intelsat currently has a fleet of over 20 high-powered spacecraft in geostationary orbit, and its Operations Center (IOC) is in Washington DC. But it is not the largest operator.

SES Global
Following the acquisition of GE Americom by SES in 2001, SES Global has a fleet of 42 satellites at the time of writing. However, not all of these satellites are available for SNG – some are exclusively for DTH broadcasting. The GE Americom fleet of satellites holds a dominant position in North America.

PanAmSat
Originally the first privately owned international satellite operator with the launch of its first satellite in 1987, PanAmSat merged with the Hughes Communications Galaxy domestic US satellite system in 1996, to form a global fleet to challenge Intelsat. PanAmSat now has a fleet of 23 satellites in orbit, and its IOC (International Operations Center) is in Homestead, Florida.

Eutelsat
The European Telecommunications Satellite Organisation (Eutelsat) was founded in 1977 to develop a European regional satellite system. Originally membership criteria for countries were that they were a sovereign state, European and a member of the ITU. Eutelsat was formally established as an inter-governmental organization in 1985. While Eutelsat is nominally a regional satellite operator, its fleet of 19 satellites span North America in the west to India in the east, so in reality it is a supra-regional operator. Like Intelsat, Eutelsat privatized in July 2001, with telecommunications and media companies from 48 different countries as shareholders.

Eutelsat's control centre (CSC) is in Paris. As with Intelsat, Eutelsat requires uplinks wishing to operate onto their capacity to fulfil performance criteria similar to Intelsat, and be registered with them.

Other operators
Satellite operators constitute a dynamic business, made even more challenging by consolidation and new entrants, globalization and the search for more added value in service provision. This in turn is applying pressure on spectrum, and the result of this is that the number of geostationary satellites is increasing, with virtually all the satellite system operators expanding their fleets. There is also an increasing number of mergers and strategic alliances being formed to try to dominate as much of the market as possible.

Europe

The European market is smaller than the North American market, with SES Astra and Eutelsat being the primary operators for the region. France Telecom operates the Telecom series of satellites, Loral operates Europe*Star, Spanish operator Hispasat operates the Hispasat series and Norwegian operator Telenor operates the Thor series. Some of these companies also operate capacity on Intelsat and Eutelsat capacity, but all are important providers for SNG capacity within Europe. However, without doubt the principal SNG space segment provider within Europe is Eutelsat.

Other regional satellite operators

In other regions of the world, there are a number of regional systems, some of which are wholly or partially owned by some of the global operators.

In the Middle East and North Africa region, the principal regional providers are Arabsat, Nilesat and Turksat.

In the Asia-Pacific region, the principal regional providers are AsiaSat, Apstar and JCSAT.

In South America, Nahuelsat operates a private commercial satellite system covering Argentina and other Latin-American countries, while the Solidaridad satellites cover Central America.

It is difficult to adequately cover the current situation in a book as satellites are launched and taken out of service. All you need to remember is that within virtually any region, space segment resource is generally available from either a regional or a global satellite operator.

Satellite operators

The use of satellite capacity

We have now reached the point where we can look at the different types of satellite capacity available, and how satellite capacity is actually accessed. SNG can be used across all types of capacity, but we will look at occasional capacity in particular.

The price structure of capacity, whether it is occasional, long- or short-term lease, pre-emptible or non-pre-emptible, is determined on at least the following four parameters:

(1) period required
(2) bandwidth
(3) power
(4) geographical coverage.

Satellite capacity can be bought for periods from 10 min to 15 years, and this describes the range of services from occasional to long-term lease.

Bandwidth can be bought from a 100 kHz to 150 MHz. For analogue video, the smallest bandwidth channel is 17 MHz, and the largest is 36 MHz, with 27 MHz being a typical channel size. For digital video, the data rate of the channel is usually between 3 and 24 Mbps, with typically 3–6 Mbps for video distribution to cable TV head-ends (distribution points), 4–8 Mbps for news contributions and 8–24 Mbps for sports and events.

Bandwidth is not the only significant parameter on a satellite – there is also the issue of the power required from the satellite, as this is a factor which is one of the key parameters in determining the life of a satellite. If a large amount of transmitted power is required from the satellite to the ground, this will affect the pricing. Similarly (and this is particularly relevant to SNG) if the satellite channel has to have increased gain in the receive stage (to be more 'sensitive') this will also affect the pricing. Finally, capacity is priced according to the beam coverage required. There are different beam patterns depending on the frequency band, and the precise geographical coverage is defined.

In the Ku-band, there are 'spotbeams' and widebeams (also called broad-beams, 'superbeams' or, in Europe, Eurobeams); while in the C-band there are global and hemi-beams.

Spotbeams usually cover an area approximately 3000 km (2000 miles) in diameter, though this can vary from satellite to satellite, and is determined by the design of the antennas of the satellite. Spot beams are often 'shaped' to cover landmasses rather than oceans, as obviously the landmass is where signals need to be concentrated.

Ku-band widebeams offer broader coverage, perhaps 8000 km (5000 miles) in diameter, but are only available at lower power levels because the power is spread over a wider area.

In the C-band, a global beam is a wide area low-power beam that covers a significant amount of the Earth's surface – although plainly it is impossible for a beam to literally cover the whole of the globe. In fact, a global beam symmetrically covers just less than half the hemisphere, with the centre of the beam often centred on the Equator.

A hemi-beam is a C-band beam that covers approximately half the area of a global beam, and might typically cover a continent, or straddle parts of two continents to provide inter-continental connectivity, and is therefore 'shaped'. It is a higher power beam than the global beam because the power is more focussed onto a specific area.

Each satellite has a defined area of coverage, both for the uplink and the downlink, and the satellite operator defines these in planning a service from a satellite before it has even been launched. The coverage is published by the satellite operator in the form of 'footprints', which show the geographical coverage of each of the uplink and the downlink beams from the satellite.

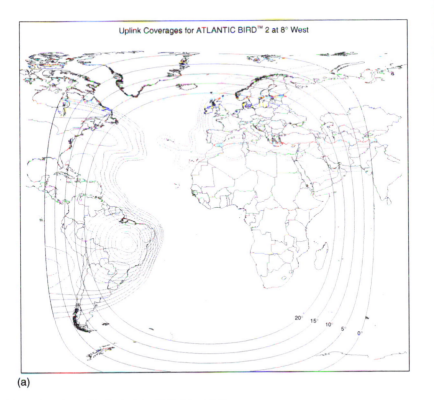

(a)

Examples of satellite footprints (© Eutelsat SA)

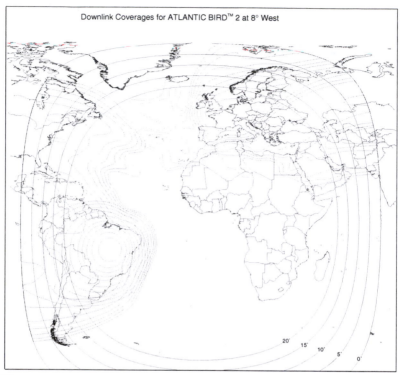

Downlink Coverages for ATLANTIC BIRD™ 2 at 8° West

(b)

Examples of satellite footprints (© Eutelsat SA)

Types of capacity

Satellite capacity is broadly divided into distribution and contribution. Distribution capacity is used to deliver signals to cable head-ends or transmitters for terrestrial distribution, or for DTH satellite delivery. Contribution capacity provides routes for transmitting material from point-to-point (generally) for inclusion in distributed programmes after (usually) some production process.

There are several different types of satellite capacity that can be accessed by SNG uplinks, and satellite system operators broadly classify these as follows:

■ dedicated/non-dedicated
■ long-/short-term leasing
■ occasional
■ inclined orbit.

The type of capacity determines, in a number of ways, the method of working for an SNG uplink (this is true whether it is a truck or flyaway system). An uplink can access capacity which covers a number of the above types – for instance, it could have a booking for 'occasional', 'dedicated' capacity, which might be in inclined orbit.

Dedicated and non-dedicated capacity

The term used for capacity on a satellite that has been specifically set aside for a particular purpose is dedicated capacity. So for instance, on Intelsat and Eutelsat satellites, there is dedicated capacity allocated individually for services such as business data, video, audio and radio services, public telephony, paging and messaging, and Internet.

The reason why there is a separation of capacity into dedicated uses is that this allows the satellite operator to optimize the technical parameters of a transponder (or group of transponders) providing a particular service. For instance, a satellite operator may concentrate DTH services on one particular satellite, so that consumers can have their satellite dishes pointed at a single satellite only for a wide range of channels.

SNG places particular demands on the satellite operator. SNG signals tend to be made up of a number of relatively short duration signals of differing power levels, with transmissions starting and ending in an apparently random sequence. Therefore, it too tends to be grouped onto a particular transponder or group of transponders on a satellite. This allows the cycle of transmissions frequently beginning and ending from possibly interfering with other services.

There is an increasing amount of capacity allocated for SNG purposes, which is kept available for occasional traffic. Often the capacity allocated to occasional SNG traffic is capacity not normally required for any other purpose, so non-dedicated capacity is spare capacity that can be used for SNG or any other temporary use on occasions if it is available. Every satellite operator always has some spare capacity available to accommodate in-service failures on satellites, and if the circumstances are right, this capacity may become available for SNG. For instance, if an important news story breaks in a particular area, satellite operators may be prepared to offer capacity not committed to some other service for SNG. It has even been known for a satellite operator to 'shuffle' services around to create suitable capacity for SNG, if they perceive that there may be a significant financial advantage (due to demand) in offering SNG short-term capacity on a story.

Capacity may also change from dedicated to non-dedicated at various times. This may be a transponder, or a part-transponder, that is vacant in between the ending of one long-term lease (also sometimes called a full-time lease) and the beginning of the next.

Short-term leases

These are available for short periods – usually one to four weeks – and short-term leases are particularly popular where a major news or sporting event is taking place in an area where interested broadcasters and newsgatherers do not already have leased capacity available. A number of satellite operators made capacity especially available for the Winter Olympic Games in Nagano, Japan in 1996, the 'hand over' of Hong Kong in 1997, the Gulf crisis in early 1998, the 1998 World Cup Football, the Sydney Olympics in 2000 and the aftermath of the terrorist attacks on the United States in 2001.

Short-term leases offered on this type of capacity are charged at a higher pro rata rate than long-term leases.

Occasional capacity

This type of capacity is typically used for SNG operations, but occasional (ad hoc) capacity is scarce in some areas of the world, and relatively plentiful in others. For most newsgatherers, the availability of occasional 'on-demand' capacity is critical. Even though a newsgathering organization may have leased capacity, a story can break in an area out of the geographical service area of their leased capacity, or create such a demand for feeds that extra capacity needs to be bought in. Smaller newsgatherers may depend totally on being able to access occasional capacity, whether they are global or regional newsgatherers, and this is an important market for satellite operators. However, whenever there is a big news story in a poorly served area, it is often a struggle for satellite operators to meet the demand.

The relative cost of occasional capacity is high in comparison to leased capacity, but it is reasonable when considering the extra work that a satellite operator has to undertake to meet occasional service requests. Bookings are usually of a minimum 10 min duration, extendible in 1 or 5 min increments. It is not unusual for a booking to be placed at less than 15 min notice.

There are high cancellation charges, which are factored depending on how much notice is given before the booking is cancelled. Virtually all satellite operators will demand 100% payment with less than 24 hours notice of cancellation. However, discounts are given for regular periodic bookings, or for a commitment to use a given number of hours of capacity in a month.

Inclined orbit

Satellites of interest for newsgathering purposes are in a geostationary orbit, but the process of sustaining a perfectly maintained geostationary orbit cannot be continued indefinitely. 'Station-keeping' manoeuvres consume energy on board the satellite that cannot be replenished, as the thruster motors that correct the position and altitude of the satellite consume the finite reserves of liquid fuel. At a certain point in the life of a satellite, a decision is taken to abandon some station-keeping manoeuvres, as they are not critical to sustaining the correct orbit. When certain station-keeping is abandoned, the satellite is said to be in inclined orbit.

Essentially, as the satellite is 'observed' from the Earth's surface, it no longer appears to be stationary in relation to that point on the Earth's surface, and requires tracking by both the SNG uplink as well as the downlink earth station. When there is insufficient fuel to even sustain basic station-keeping, the satellite is deemed to be finally terminated and is declared as being at the end of life. Capacity that is completely station-kept – i.e. stable – commands a higher premium than capacity deemed to be in inclined orbit. The disadvantage of inclined-orbit capacity is that the SNG has to constantly track the path of inclination. At the downlink, where the receiving antenna is fairly large (over 3.5 m), this is commonly performed by auto-tracking equipment, which not only gradually moves the antenna to keep the satellite on-beam, but also 'learns' the daily cycle so that it is able to predict the direction to move the antenna. In terms of SNG uplink, this tracking has to be performed manually.

Hence this capacity is available at lower cost on satellites that are in the final phase of their operational life. In fact, inclined orbit capacity is attractive for SNG, as the majority of transmissions are point-to-point and typically of short duration, and therefore the particular characteristics of an inclined-orbit satellite can easily be coped with by an experienced SNG operator.

Types of capacity

Operating an SNG uplink

We have not discussed what qualifications or training a person operating an SNG uplink needs to have. Amazingly, considering the potential damage that an uplink can cause both to the satellite and to the people in the vicinity of the SNG uplink (as we shall see when we look at safety issues), there is no qualification required to operate a satellite uplink in virtually any country in the world. In general, neither governments nor satellite operators demand that operators should have undertaken specific satellite operations training or reached a defined level of competence before being allowed to switch an uplink into transmit.

The emphasis is, and always has been, on the equipment meeting very stringent technical requirements, but no parallel requirements for the operators. Consequently, the majority of training is 'on the job', and the company operating the uplink allows an individual to operate an uplink when they are satisfied that the operator is competent. There are only a few specific training courses in SNG uplink operations.

Placing a booking for occasional space segment

Having obtained satellite system registration for the uplink, deployed the uplink to the location of the story with skilled operators and secured whatever licence or permission is required to operate, the process of securing satellite capacity (assuming you are not working onto your own lease) should have already begun.

To find and book occasional capacity segment there is a process that has to be followed, step-by-step. In many parts of the world, finding and booking space segment is like shopping around for any other commonly traded commodity, particularly where there is a thriving competitive market to provide space segment.

Before seeking capacity, the operator will need to obtain a suitable licence or permission from the National Administration of the country of operation. Having obtained this, or at least begun the process, there are a number of basic parameters that need to be established:

- the location where the uplink is going to operate
- the registration identity of the SNG uplink for the relevant satellite systems
- certain basic technical parameters of the SNG uplink – power, antenna size/gain, Ku- or C-band, analogue or digital
- the date and time for transmission
- the downlink details.

As previously mentioned, capacity is normally bought on the basis of a minimum booking of 10 min transmission, with extra time being bought on one or 5 min increments. Often a 5 min allowance is given prior to the transmission for technical line-up, provided there is time available on that particular channel/transponder.

In DSNG we speak of 'booking a channel' for a transmission. For digital SNG transmissions, where it is common for data rate of 8 Mbps to be used, a satellite transponder can be subdivided into a number of channels, typically 9 MHz wide. As a very rough rule of thumb, in 2003 an 8 Mbps digital channel costs around US$10 per minute.

Certainly in the United States and Europe, the process of purchasing capacity is essentially very simple. Armed with the required information, as above, it is a matter of telephoning service providers, whether system operators or satellite segment brokers, and placing the enquiry. In highly developed markets, the whole process of seeking offers and deciding as to which suits best in either price or service can be achieved in under an hour, virtually around the clock.

Before finally committing to using the capacity, there will probably be a requirement to provide the national radiocommunications administration with the details of the transmission for frequency clearance or as a condition of the terms of the licence or permission.

Multi- and unilateral operations

When a satellite transmission is from point-to-point, it is described as a unilateral transmission. This is the typical SNG transmission from an uplink in the field back to a single destination such as a broadcaster's studio. Where a transmission is from one origin to a number of destinations simultaneously, this is called a 'multilateral' transmission. In the TV news environment, examples of multilaterals are the daily news exchanges between members of broadcasting unions, e.g. Eurovison (EBU) and Asiavison (ABU), where news material shot by one member is offered up for sharing with other members – a type of news co-operative.

Pools

Another type of multilateral is where an uplink is providing pool material to a number of clients. A pool is where a group of newsgatherers agree to share pictures and/or resources on a story for common use, and a pool may be set up for a number of reasons. A number of broadcasters and news agencies have standing arrangements to share material with each other, and some similar arrangements exist between individual broadcasters. The purpose is usually either to save cost, or because access to a particular news event has been granted on the basis that material will be shot by one camera crew and pooled with other interested parties.

Operating an SNG uplink

Safety

The operation of terrestrial microwave and satellite uplinks unfortunately brings both the operator and occasionally the public into contact with a number of potential hazards. So we need to examine the range of hazards and the measures that can be taken to minimize the risks. There is health and safety legislation in many countries covering these hazards, and in the United Kingdom, the primary safety agency is the Health and Safety Executive (HSE).

The most important consideration when operating any type of microwave link is safety – there is a saying in the business, 'no story is worth a life'. To consider the impact on the operation it is necessary to identify the specific risks. As we are going to look at risks and hazards, let us remind ourselves of the definition of risk and hazard, as occasionally there is confusion in their usage.

A hazard is anything that can cause harm – for example, electricity is a hazard associated with electronic equipment. Risk is the chance, whether high or low, that somebody will be harmed by the hazard – for example, how much of a chance is there that someone will be electrocuted in either operating or being close to an SNG uplink. It is important that the hazards and risks are clearly identified for two reasons. First, a human injury or life may depend on the correct action being taken, and secondly, the owner and/or operator of the microwave equipment may be liable to prosecution for failing to identify the hazards and take suitable steps to minimize the risks.

Outline of hazards
There are a number of potential hazards encountered when operating microwave links – whether terrestrial or satellite:

- non-ionizing radiation
- electrical hazards
- operating pneumatic masts
- manual handling issues
- working at heights
- driving of vehicles
- operating in hostile environments, including war zones.

Non-ionizing radiation
As we talked about earlier in the book, microwave radiation can be used to heat organic matter up – and the word 'radiation' usually instils people with fear.

One of the first lessons anyone has to learn when being involved with the use of microwave transmitters is the hazard of radiation – but it is non-ionizing radiation, which is significantly different to ionizing radiation. So to dispel some myths, let us be clear about the differences between ionizing and non-ionizing radiation.

Ionizing radiation is radiation emitted by X-rays, gamma rays, neutrons and alpha particles that has sufficient energy to knock electrons out of atoms and thus ionize them. When this radiation passes through the tissues of a living body, in amounts above a safe level, then there is sufficient energy to permanently alter cell structures and damage DNA. This in turn can have dramatic and potentially catastrophic effects on living tissue, including, of course, human beings. However, used in controlled doses, ionizing radiation is widely used as a medical diagnostic and treatment tool, and provided the doses are within acceptable limits and there are adequate precautions to minimize the risk, there is little to fear from such use.

This is not the type of radiation associated with microwave-transmitting equipment. Microwave-transmitting equipment – which of course includes terrestrial microwave links, Inmarsat satphones and SNG uplinks – emits non-ionizing radiation. In the following discussion on non-ionizing radiation, the term microwave transmitter can be taken to include the whole range of link equipment we have talked about.

The definition of non-ionizing radiation is electromagnetic radiation, which encompasses the spectrum of ultraviolet radiation, light, infrared radiation and RF radiation (including radio waves and microwaves). This is of much lower energy than ionizing radiation and therefore is unable to knock electrons out of atoms. When this type of radiation passes through the tissues of the body it does not have sufficient energy to ionize biologically important atoms, and therefore to alter cell structures or damage DNA. However, it does have thermal effects, and frequencies in the range 30–300 MHz have the greatest effect as the human body can more easily absorb them. At frequencies above this range, the body absorption is less, but still may be significant if the power levels are high enough.

Thermal effects are considered the primary health risk of non-ionizing radiation. The absorption of RF energy varies with frequency. Microwave frequencies produce a skin effect – you can literally sense your skin starting to feel warm if you are exposed to high power levels at microwave frequencies – but the real damage is happening deep inside your body. After all, as we said earlier, this is the principle on which microwave ovens operate, and you can cook human tissue just as easily with this type of power as animal tissue. While the terrestrial microwave links we have looked at can work very near to the same frequency as microwave ovens, why is there a problem with satellite uplinks operating at 14 GHz? Well, even the high levels of energy given off at this frequency could potentially cause some heating effects in the human body under the right conditions – standing directly in front of the antenna being the most obvious.

RF radiation may penetrate the body and be absorbed in deep body organs without the skin effect, which can warn an individual of danger. This is called deep burning, and there are certain parts of the human body that are particularly sensitive to these deep heating effects – the eyes, and additionally in males, the testicles. Therefore, power levels around microwave-transmitting equipment need to be kept below a certain level to minimize the risk to people.

Preferably, people need to be kept away from the most dangerous parts of this equipment, especially the antenna, which is designed to focus all this energy in a particular direction.

Dealing with hazards with microwave equipment

The most hazardous area when operating microwave links is in front of the antenna. This is a particular problem with SNG flyaways and transportable Inmarsat satphones as they are often placed on the ground, or operated so that the beam is at a height through which people may pass. It is less of an issue with SNG and ENG trucks, where the antenna is mounted either on the roof or at least high up on the vehicle structure, and hence out of harms way.

It is not necessarily a lower risk with a smaller rather than a larger antenna, as the potential hazard is directly related to the output power delivered from the antenna, which is related to the size of the HPA as well as the antenna. However, it is recognized that as an SNG antenna is directional, the area of risk can be clearly defined.

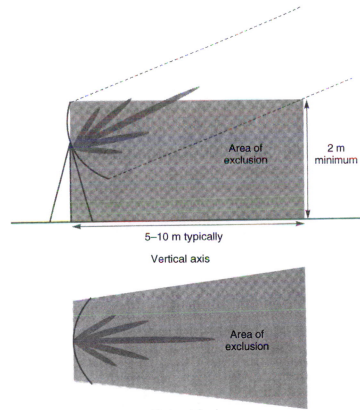

Area of risk from non-ionizing radiation

This makes the task of reducing the risk to manageable proportions much more viable, even in a public area. However, the amount of power is effectively focussed into a high power beam, and significantly high power can be measured even from a considerable distance away from the antenna in the direction of the satellite. Incidentally, this creates a secondary risk relating to aircraft, as we shall see later.

SNG antennas are highly directional, and therefore the likelihood of significant human exposure to non-ionizing radiation is considerably reduced. Nevertheless, the potential for exposure must take into account the following:

- the direction (azimuth and elevation) the SNG antenna is pointing
- its height above the ground
- its location relative to where both the public and the uplink operators may pass
- the operational procedures followed to minimize the risks.

When calculating and applying the limits, consideration needs to be taken of the potential time of exposure. The limits set by UK safety agencies are set within a limited time frame of exposure, but in practice, it is wise to apply these limits as if they relate to an instantaneous exposure. By doing so, any operator is going to be erring on the side of safety.

The position in the United Kingdom

In the United Kingdom, the National Radiological Protection Board (NRPB) is responsible for research and advising best practice in the area of radiation hazards, including non-ionizing radiation. It was established in 1970, and the current recommendations were revised in 1993.

The NRPB makes no distinction in exposure levels between the general public and the workers involved in RF transmission (unlike the US). It also does not define absolute limits, but sets 'investigation' levels, above which adverse biological effects are likely to occur. Exceeding these investigation levels does not automatically infer biological damage will occur, but that further biological investigation may be necessary and is recommended.

It also uses different methods of measurement depending on the frequency band concerned. Within the frequency bands of interest to us, it has an exposure level for 100 kHz–10 GHz, and a different level for 10–300 GHz, averaged over a certain period.

The limit is 10 mW/cm^2 power density on any part of the body – for a Ku-band uplink, the averaging period approximates to just over 4 min. Because of the problems of measuring body absorption below 10 GHz, it is not easy to give a definitive level, though the averaging period is 15 min.

The position in the United States

In the United States, the Federal Communications Commission (FCC) defines maximum permissible exposure (MPE) limits, and their policy is not as straightforward as that in the United Kingdom. There are two limits, one set for members

174

of the general public (General Population), and the other for workers involved in operating and maintaining RF-transmitting equipment (Occupational).

The MPE for General Population exposure for the frequency range 1.5–100 GHz, which encompasses all ENG and SNG frequencies, is 1 mW/cm^2, averaged over a 30-min period. The FCC deems that General Population (i.e. uncontrolled) exposures apply where the general public may be exposed, or where workers may not be fully aware of the potential for exposure, or cannot exercise control over their exposure.

The MPE for Occupational exposure, which allows a higher exposure limit for the same frequency range, is 5 mW/cm^2, averaged over a 6-min period. Occupational (i.e. controlled) limits apply where workers are exposed provided they are fully aware of the potential for exposure and can exercise control over the degree of their exposure.

Practical steps to minimize risks

What are the practical steps that can be taken to minimize the risk to both operator and general public? Assuming that the antenna and the transmitting equipment are in an area to which either the operator or a member of the public has access, i.e. it is not mounted on a vehicle roof, then there are essentially simple measures which can usually be taken which will give reasonable protection.

In order of importance, they are:

- rigging the microwave transmitter and antenna in a restricted access area
- cordoning-off of a 'safety zone', and providing warning signs
- in the case of an SNG uplink, check measurements around the perimeter of the safety zone
- restricting access
- supervising and checking during transmissions.

Obviously, the risk of exposure particularly for members of the general public, can be greatly minimized if the link can be rigged in a position which has secure access while also meeting the operational requirements. This is not always possible, but if it can be achieved then the risk of exposure is limited to the link operator. Unfortunately time and logistics can conspire against achieving this aim, particularly in a breaking news story situation.

Safety zones

The idea of the safety zone is to protect anyone from entering an area where there is a likelihood of non-ionizing radiation 'spillage' for the antenna. A zone should be cordoned off around the front and side areas of the antenna. The limit of this safety zone depends on three factors – the angle of elevation of the antenna, the operating band of the link and the maximum output power capable of being delivered from the antenna.

The best way of determining this area is by using a non-ionizing radiation field strength meter, and the most practical form of this is a 'personal protection badge' with an audible and visual alarm, available at a relatively moderate cost.

Dealing with hazards with microwave equipment

Having set the elevation angle of the antenna, a generous distance should be allowed and cordoned off – up to 10 m if possible for an SNG uplink. Once a satellite uplink is transmitting, the operator can then check that at the perimeter of this safety zone the exposure level is below the limit defined. Obviously, if a flyaway is sited on a rooftop, pointing out over the side of the building, then there is little likelihood of anyone being able to stray in front of the antenna!

The operator should keep an eye on any movement of people near the perimeter, and try to be vigilant in ensuring that nobody attempts to stray inside the safety zone perimeter. Signs warning of a risk should also be placed at the perimeter, and international pictogram signs are available that depict the hazard.

At regular intervals throughout an operation, the zone perimeter, the waveguides and flange joints should be checked to ensure that the operation continues to be safe, both for the operator and the general public.

Risk to the operator

It should be noted at this point that we have so far concentrated on the risk of exposure from the antenna. However, there is also a risk of non-ionizing radiation leaking from the waveguide and its connection between the output flange of the HPA and the input flange of the antenna feed. This is particularly true of flexible waveguides, which although flexible, deteriorate over time with the flexing of the waveguide from rigging and de-rigging the flyaway equipment. The waveguide should be regularly inspected for physical signs of wear, cuts or burn marks (hot spots), which are an early indication of impending failure (these marks may be noticed as a series of evenly spaced transverse marks along the length of the waveguide).

(a) Flexible waveguides; (b) Rigid waveguides

Operations near airports

In the United Kingdom, the Civil Aviation Authority (CAA) considers that the high energy beam from an SNG antenna operating in the Ku-band could cause a serious malfunction in an aircraft's instrumentation if the aircraft passed too close through the uplink beam. For example, this might apply if an aircraft, on approach or take-off, was to fly through the beam from an uplink that is only a few kilometres away. There are strict requirements from the UK Radiocommunications Agency (RA) in the operation of SNG uplinks near airports. There are no such restrictions in relation to temporary ENG terrestrial microwave links.

In the United Kingdom and many other countries, operation near or at military installations is restricted, although special clearance may be obtained. This may be justified on either the grounds of potential EMI or security.

There are strong electromagnetic fields from military systems, and it is not unusual for this to have an effect on the camera rather than the SNG uplink. Radar in particular (as it produces very large but short pulses of RF) can affect the pictures, resulting on analogue cameras as black line flashing or on the now more common digital cameras, strange disturbances such as broad bands in the picture colour.

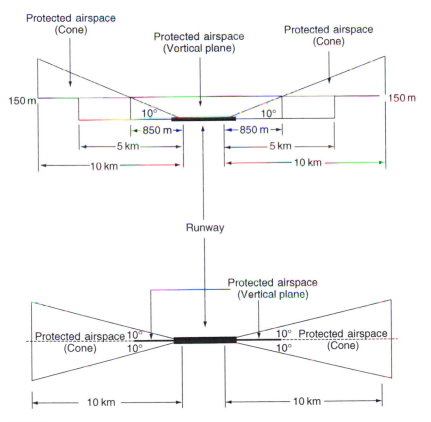

UK RA Safety zone at airports

Electrical hazards

As with any electrical equipment, electrical power has to be supplied to make the equipment function. It would be preferable if this power could be provided from low power batteries, hence minimizing hazards associated with electrical power. However, in general, microwave equipment needs more power than can be provided from batteries. Some small ENG trucks can be powered from batteries topped up from the vehicle alternator when the vehicle is driving, but it is more usual to use a generator.

In particular, the demand for primary supply power for an SNG uplink and all the associated equipment is quite high, even for a small system. Typically, an SNG uplink requires at least 3 kW, and large SNG systems require at least 6 kW. This can only be derived from AC power, and therefore there are hazards in operating SNG equipment related not only to the power source itself, but also to the condition of the equipment.

Rugged extremes

It has to be borne in mind the type of rugged life the equipment leads, as well as the exposure to widely varying weather conditions, which over time can cause a deterioration in the electrical integrity of the equipment itself unless it is regularly checked by competent technicians. SNG uplinks can be operated in desert conditions, with temperatures reaching over 50 °C; in tropical conditions, with relative humidity over 90%; or in very cold conditions, with the temperature reaching −30 °C.

There is an added hazard in that the amplifying element typically used in most SNG HPAs – the travelling wave tube (TWT) – requires a very high voltage supply, which although generated internally in the HPA is nevertheless a potential hazard. Some of the monitoring equipment also have high voltage supplies, so all the equipment in a system is vulnerable.

Taking care

Regular care of the equipment, as well as respect in its use, is vital to minimize the risks. But care also has to be taken in where you get the supply of power. Generally, the uplink operator can either obtain power from a local supply, or more likely, transport a generator (usually petrol) along with the system. With a truck-based operation, using vehicles built for the purpose, this is relatively straightforward and very professional, and safe power systems are installed in these vehicles. They usually incorporate various safety features to ensure minimal risk to people and equipment.

With a flyaway operation, the situations are usually much more difficult. It is common to transport a system with its own generator, as one never knows if there is an adequate power supply at the destination – if there is one at all. Having arrived at the location, assuming the local supply is not reliable or safe enough (often the case in areas where flyaways are typically deployed), the generator has to be placed in a convenient position. Some thought also has to be given to re-fuelling arrangements (including the safe storage of fuel) as well as the safe routing of cable from the generator to the uplink equipment.

The residual current device (RCD)

Finally, it is worth considering the use of a residual current device (RCD) in the supply to the uplink equipment. An RCD is a safety device that monitors the power supply constantly checking for a fault – we discussed these earlier. It does not act as an over-current circuit breaker or fuse, which protects the circuit from drawing too much current beyond the capacity of the cable and the equipment, but is an additional safety device.

The advantage of the RCD is that it does not require a good earth connection, or any earth connection at all for that matter, to operate. It will protect people even with the most basic electrical supply being available, and is compact, cheap and easy to use.

Residual current device (RCD)

Operating ENG pneumatic masts

As we saw earlier, ENG trucks inevitably have a pneumatic mast, and this brings us to a hazard that is peculiar to ENG microwave – that of raising the mast. The hazards we have spoken of already are real enough, but of all the equipment we discuss in this book, the most potentially hazardous is not the microwave antenna, or the electrical supply, but the pneumatic mast. The raising of a 40 foot plus pole vertically into the air places a heavy burden of responsibility on the operator.

Overhead hazards

In the United States raising a mast into overhead cables is a too common incident, due to the fact that there are a lot of ENG microwave vans in use, with operators who often have not been trained properly, and working for stations who do not place enough emphasis on safety training. Too much emphasis is on 'getting the story back' – at whatever cost.

In addition, the situation is exacerbated because in the United States much of the power distribution in cities is above ground – too much power on poles that should be a lot higher, in the wrong places, and at too high a voltage.

Look up!

The golden rule in operating masts on vans is 'Look up!'. Always check before you raise the mast that there is nothing above that the mast is likely to become entangled with – and it is a good idea to keep at least 3 m away from any power lines – and 6 m if it is a very high voltage line. In the United Kingdom, lines carrying 240 or 415 V are common on rural roads. Supplies to farms are typically 11 kV. The huge pylons you see marching across the countryside are carrying 132 and 400 kV. The big difference in the United Kingdom is the way our power is distributed, compared to the United States. In UK cities power in urban and metropolitan areas is almost exclusively distributed underground, so it is only in the countryside that it is on poles. In the United Kingdom very high voltage lines are kept well clear of roads, etc., wherever possible.

The second rule is always check the mast is fully down before driving away. Sounds obvious – well, it has happened countless times – in the hurry to get packed up and off to the next story – that the mast gets forgotten about, and the operator drives the vehicle away with a 40 foot pole sticking out of the top of the vehicle.

In the United Kingdom we have been relatively lucky in there having been to date few accidents of this nature – but this should not make us complacent about this issue.

An excellent ENG safety website – www.engsafety.com – lists the known incidents with masts on ENG vehicles in the United States – along with a lot of useful safety information. Many such accidents involved technicians and reporters sustaining serious injuries, including amputation of limbs through severe electrocution burns, and even fatalities. There are on average three reported incidents each year in the United States but it is reckoned that the actual number of incidents is probably around three hundred per annum. As Mark Bell (who runs www.engsafety.com) wisely comments, 'Accident numbers are only the bad luck, not the actual numbers of incidents. You always have to keep in mind that the only difference between an accident and a catastrophe is luck.'

Anatomy of an ENG accident

The following is an account written by Gary Stigall, an engineer at KFMB-TV in Los Angeles, taken from Mark Bell's website. It makes sobering reading.

'At a few minutes before ten on the morning of Monday 22 May 2000, the KFMB-TV assignment editor called over the intercom in an urgent tone, "Could you dial in Telstar Six, One Delta?" The transmissions person was on lunch break. I went into transmissions and hit the screen button that would command the satellite receiver to change channels. What we began to see made us all stop our work.

Unsteady cameras showed us that something terrible had happened to a news van. We heard murmurings about "Adrienne". The Channel Two photographer was interviewing a mechanic who had witnessed the accident in Hollywood.

I will try to reconstruct the scene in the interest of exploring what happened when a KABC-TV news van microwave dish brushed a power line in Holly-wood, burning reporter Adrienne Alpert over 25% of her body. This reconstruc-tion is based on the raw tape and live video I watched from KCBS-TV, from the descriptions of witnesses on the scene, and from friends of people there.

At about 9:40 that Monday morning, photographer Heather MacKenzie and reporter Adrienne Alpert arrived at a Hollywood location on Santa Monica Boulevard where they would join other news crews to report on a story about child car seat safety. They apparently agreed that the location they had first chosen to park was directly under the power lines, so they moved to a location a few feet away, adjoining a shop. However, the location chosen has a pro-nounced slope downward toward the street, where they had just come from.

Heather must have started the generator and air compressor. The mast is a telescoping air tank, rising when pressurized. The controls were in an industry standard location, just inside the rear doors. When the lever is raised, air flows from storage tank and compressor to the mast. Heather must have opened the doors and began raising the mast. Since the van sat on a slope, the mast was listing from vertical. The photographs taken show that the driver side of the van was within a foot or two of being directly underneath some 34 500 V lines. Above those lines were perhaps a dozen higher voltage lines. This is a busy trunk of electricity.

At some time, Heather went inside the truck where Adrienne sat, and called in to begin transmitting and steering the dish to a relay site. Witnesses, including a couple of mechanics working near where the two had parked, said they began yelling at the two from outside to stop the raising mast. A crew across the street from channel 62 started videotaping the mast as it brushed the wires, and apparently they, too, yelled and waved.

The two women decided to get out of the van's passenger side doors. Adrienne Alpert stepped out of the van. At that second, the circuit completed from the 34 500 volt line, arcing through the top of the parabolic dish to its inner reflective mesh, to its mount, to the aluminium mast, to the van body, its door handle, from her left hand through her body to her right foot. The van was parked so near the building that the door apparently struck the wall. A nearby drain pipe, perhaps filled with air conditioner condensate, is seen in several after shots with a large char mark where the pipe enters the steel mesh-filled stucco wall. The pavement is wet where the water has been draining near the front of the van. Whether Adrienne stepped on wet ground is not clear. When the door hit the wall, the main explosion apparently occurred.

Whether her windpipes had been burned or her diaphragm had been paralysed, she began having trouble breathing and asked for help. Bystanders wanted to assist, but were not sure whether they were clear of electrocution danger yet. The mast came down from the wires rapidly, the seals having now failed.

The closed circuit feed showed horrible burns on Adrienne's limbs. As of the date of this writing, she has undergone amputations of the left forearm and right leg below the knee. Heather was not injured.'

This account should make us all pause and reflect – and recite again the mantra 'No Story Is Worth A Life'.

Unfortunately, in the United States there have been a string of such incidents over the last two decades – many of them are chronicled on www.engsafety.com. It may not only be the operator in the truck who is injured or killed – the cameraman on the end of the cable connected to the truck is just as vulnerable in the event of a mast touching overhead cables.

There are other potential hazards with masts as well. There have been a number of incidents where sections of the mast have 'launched' – the tube seals fail and the build-up of pressure fires a section of the mast into the air. This can lead to the frightening prospect of a metal tube hurtling to the ground with a head load of antenna and microwave amplifier in excess of 50 kg.

The pressure of time

Without doubt, however, no matter where the SNG or ENG truck is being driven, the greatest hazard the operator faces is time pressure. Particularly on a breaking story, there is an inherent pressure on the operator to get to the location as quickly as possible to get on air. This pressure may or may not be directly applied – but it is always there. Operators need to exercise considerable self-discipline in order that this pressure does not affect their driving. Stress and fatigue are the two most likely causes of a vehicle accident, both of which are common in working in newsgathering.

Mast safety alarms

There is help at hand in helping detect overhead cables above and beyond your own eyes. There are several products on the market that are designed to detect overhead cables. These essentially detect the electric field radiated from power cables and will both sound an alarm and open the valve on the pneumatic mast, dumping all the air out and so lowering the mast. These devices are effective, and their use is to be encouraged.

DANGER

DO NOT OPERATE
WITHIN 10 FT. OF
POWER LINES

Sign seen in every US ENG truck

Three basic rules:

(1) Check the area above before beginning to raise the mast – power cable within 3 m? – DON'T RAISE THE MAST.
(2) If it is clear, still watch the mast going up – all the way.
(3) Do not forget to watch as you lower the mast – fully – at the end of the assignment.

Follow these rules and the risk of an incident – let alone an accident – will be drastically reduced.

Operating ENG pneumatic masts

Manual handling

The issue of manual handling – which is about minimizing the risk of musculo-skeletal disorders – is particularly important when looking at the use of flyaway SNG uplinks. As we have already seen, flyaway systems are typically made up of a large number of boxes, and some of these cases can be particularly heavy – each up to 75 kg. Although back injuries through lifting awkward or heavy cases do not account for work-related deaths, they do account for a significant amount of human suffering. Back disorders are one of the leading causes of disability for people in their working years, and SNG and ENG operators quite commonly suffer some degree of discomfort from back pain caused by lifting during their work.

Back problems can either be caused by a single traumatic incident, or more often through a gradual process of repetitive strain over a period. Because of the slow and progressive onset of this internal injury, the condition is often ignored until the symptoms become acute, often resulting in disabling injury.

Typical actions, which occur handling the SNG/ENG systems and that can lead to back injury, are:

- heavy lifting
- poor posture
- reaching, twisting or bending while lifting
- lifting with forceful movement
- poor footing.

These are further exacerbated if the operator has not been trained in correct body mechanics – how one lifts, pushes, pulls or carries objects. Additionally, poor physical condition results in losing the strength and endurance to perform physical tasks without strain.

Working on news stories almost invariably involves very long hours, varying from periods of relative inactivity interspersed with bursts of intense activity, to periods of sustained intense activity, all of which cause fatigue. Often meals are missed, sleep patterns disrupted, and dehydration can occur due to the pattern of work. If working in a different country, the operator may have to cope with changes in diet, drinking water, and perhaps effects from working across a different time zone.

Commonly, operators talk of 'landing on the ground – feet running', as their work begins immediately the moment they disembark from the aircraft. They will be directly involved in getting a very large amount of equipment through Customs and loaded into vehicles, then quickly moving to the location, and setting up the equipment as rapidly as possible. It is the nature of the business that an operation is expected to be up and running within hours of arrival, as the story is probably 'moving' and material is required for news broadcasts as quickly as possible. Once the uplink is working, of course, the work continues as the transmissions get underway.

But what does all this have to do with back injury? Quite simply, it is all too easy to forget about the weight of what you are lifting if all the pressure is on you to get those cases moved into position as quickly as possible. Local porters may be available, but invariably you will be involved in moving cases as well. If you are feeling tired due to jet lag, or just generally unwell because of the change in environment, combined with the pressure by producers to get the uplink working as quickly as possible, it is hardly surprising that even minor injuries occur. Very experienced operators, of course, have various methods of minimizing the effects of all these factors, but nonetheless back injuries are suffered by even the most experienced.

Cable safety

Associated with manual handling is the running of cables between the vehicle and the live camera position. Cables represent a trip hazard not only to operators and other crew, but may also present a serious hazard to members of the public where cables cross public areas.

There are a number of ways of minimizing the risk to everyone.

- If the cables can be lifted above ground height – 'flown' – they can be routed above peoples' heads. The difficulty can often be that in order to raise the cables above head height, to do so in itself can be hazardous.
- If the cables can only run across the ground, then they should be routed where the risk of tripping is minimized. This can be around the edge of public areas, or run along in gutters at the edge of roads (potentially unpleasant when you come to de-rig them!).
- Often they are 'matted' i.e. rubber matting is laid over the top of them so as to minimize the risk of tripping. Cables can also 'roll' when stepped upon, causing people to lose their footing. Wherever possible, cables should be matted and/or taped so as to minimize the risk of tripping.
- Running cables across roads is potentially very hazardous. Cables can get caught up in the wheels of fast-moving vehicles; a cyclist or motorcyclist can be thrown from their saddle if they hit a bunch of cables lying across a road at speed or in wet conditions. In many places, it is actually illegal to run cables across a road. This is a situation where the short-hop radio-cam link can prove invaluable in minimizing risk – and gives greatest flexibility and speed of rigging.
- Most of all, remember cables carrying mains voltages must be routed with care.

Working at heights

It is a reflection of the nature of newsgathering work that it frequently involves rapid deployment without pre-planning to areas where often you may have no detailed knowledge of local circumstances or conditions. This can be particularly problematic when you have to rig microwave or SNG equipment on roofs.

Manual handling

Below are highlighted a number of key points to consider when rigging on roofs or other 'high-points' – which can include balconies or ledges.

- It is often a good idea to wear some kind of safety harnesses which should be adequately secured at least at waist-height when working on a roof/ high-point, and including the means of access to and from the roof if it is hazardous.
- Hazardous routes to and from a roof/high-point must be treated with extreme caution, particularly when equipment is being carried up and down. You should always use appropriate safety equipment such as body harnesses where necessary, and lift the equipment by using ropes if there is not a safe way of getting the gear up to the top.
- Roofs often have surfaces coated in lichen or moss, heavy coatings of bird excrement, loose coverings – all these are potential hazards.
- Rigging over the edge of a drop even when there is an adequate barrier is potentially dangerous if equipment is being raised or lowered, as there is the risk of being pulled over the edge.
- Vertical access ladders which have no outer guard rings are a particular hazard. Any ladder higher than 3 m with no guards should have a safety line arrangement rigged on it. This will prevent falls when carrying equipment up the ladder.
- All equipment and cables once rigged on a roof/high-point need to be correctly secured so as to withstand any bad weather conditions which may prevail during the period that the rig is in place. All equipment rigged in exposed conditions should be left adequately weatherproofed for the duration of the rig.
- Any area into which any person may stray which may expose them to non-ionizing radiation generated by RF-transmitting equipment (either terrestrial microwave or satellite uplinks) must be clearly cordoned off and indicated with warning notices. This is particularly true when remotely controlled microwave link equipment is rigged.

Down below

It is just as important to pay attention to what is happening below as well. On street pavements the arrangement of a temporary barrier which will force pedestrians to walk in the roadway is not a good idea, yet on the other hand someone needs to be around on the ground to ensure that nothing happens when lifting gear up from the ground or rigging over an edge. It is a good idea to wear hard hats down below – tools have been known to be dropped! A spanner falling five floors is a fairly lethal projectile. All cables and equipment lifted to or lowered from a roof/high-point should be correctly secured and guided by a member of the crew at the base level as well as at the roof/high-point.

Streets and other public areas are a particular hazard, and it should be remembered that when a heavy weight falls it may bounce off the side of a building. Damage to a building is also avoided by guiding equipment with a rope held from below as it is pulled up or lowered.

Weather and time of day

Adverse weather conditions such as heavy rain, thick fog/mist, sleet, snow, extreme cold or conditions existing after such weather e.g. lying snow, ice or frost must be treated as a primary concern when contemplating any possible work on a roof/high-point. Conditions must be kept under constant review. The risk of accident increases dramatically even under heavy frost conditions or poor visibility and such conditions must not be underestimated. Extreme cold is a hazard in itself as it can lead to poor reactions, reduced feeling/grip, etc.

The period of dusk and dawn can be particularly risky when half-light is a positive hazard.

Checklist for working on roofs/high-points

- Is it a known site? Have you been there before?
- When is the rig to take place – day/night?
- What are the weather conditions? What have they been and what is the forecast?
- Is there enough safety equipment and of the right type loaded?
- Have all the staff who are going equipped with their personal safety equipment?
- Are there enough people going for the type of rig?
- What is the access to the roof/high-point like?
- If at night, is there lighting already there for rigging, or will temporary lights need to be rigged?
- What is the state of the surface of the working area?
- Is there an adequate barrier of safe construction?
- If not, are there suitable points for the rigging of safety lines for using safety harnesses?
- Does the area of the rig require extra vigilance and/or the erection of temporary barriers?
- Will equipment/cables be lifted to the roof/high-point?
- Will someone be in attendance top-side when the link is tested or if not have safety barriers/notices been erected?
- At the end of the rig have all equipment and cables been secured and weatherproofed if in an exposed position?

Manual handling

Working on a very dangerous glass roof!

Driving of vehicles

In both terrestrial ENG and SNG operations, driving vehicles is an intrinsic part of the job. Obviously ENG and SNG vehicles are commonly used on local stories and events, while SNG trucks are used on trans-continental events as well. Even if a system is transported by air, a truck is used to carry the equipment on the final leg of the journey to the location. The driving of vehicles is in itself a safety issue, as again the pressures of time can lead to lengthy periods spent behind the wheel, trying to navigate, and dealing with the inevitable phone calls, pager messages and other such distractions.

The only advice that can be given is that you must respect the law that often applies to driving vehicles over a certain size. Even where there is no legislation to obey, just remember that 'no story is worth a life' – and that leads us on to look at a commonly overlooked hazard of SNG/ENG operations.

Tiredness

Fatigue is a major cause of road crashes, yet the dangers of fatigue and its impact on driving are underrated. Fatigue-related accidents can occur at any time of day, but drivers need to take particular care during the mid-afternoon period and between midnight and dawn. Young drivers, shift workers, heavy vehicle drivers – some or all of which apply to drivers of newsgathering vehicles – are especially at risk of death or injury from fatigue-related crashes.

Lack of 'quality' sleep is a critical factor leading to the onset of fatigue. Ideally drivers need to be encouraged to plan their trips well in advance – unfortunately this is contrary to the nature of newsgathering.

More accidents are caused by tiredness both on the road and on site than any other factor – so be aware.

Operating in hostile environments

A hostile environment in terms of newsgathering can range from a civil riot to an international war. Operating SNG uplinks in these environments brings a new set of problems in safety and logistics. Obviously, the greatest challenge is in operating in war zones – be it a civil war, such as in Bosnia, or an international conflict as in Iraq or Afghanistan.

The greatest problems in deploying SNG systems into these situations are in both safety and logistics. But it is in these types of story that satellite transmissions from the field have had the greatest impact in shaping news bulletins, and consequently our view of significant world events.

SNG systems are typically deployed into these areas with the consideration of a large set of factors. There are the logistical elements, e.g. personnel and equipment (and money) available, and technical elements, e.g. availability of space segment to be met, and in addition all the considerations of the dangers and protective measures to be taken. These include:

- How to get to the personnel and the SNG uplink to the location?
- Assessing the level of risk to personnel – availability of personal protection equipment if required.
- Where to site the SNG uplink for minimum risk and maximum usefulness?
- How to move the SNG uplink around if necessary?
- How to get the personnel (and hopefully the equipment) out to safety in a hurry?

The immediate response

For newsgathering in hazardous or difficult and remote locations, the first major problem faced is getting into the area with a means of reporting 'live' as quickly as possible. The first 24 hours for any newsgatherer in this situation can be the most difficult, while they attempt to 'ramp up' their own resources or hire-in resources form the nearest available supplier in the region. The demand for coverage from even the most difficult and remote location is intense, particularly as there will be fierce competition from the other major newsgatherers to secure facilities for coverage.

For everyone it is very often a race as to who gets to book the nearest SNG uplink facilities, and this can be intense. In the pressure of the breaking of the story, no one can afford to spend too much time haggling over prices, as speed of reaction is just as important to the independent operator as to the client newsgatherer. Standard rate cards tend to go out of the window in these circumstances, and it becomes a matter of the highest bidder who is the fastest to the phone or fax machine.

We then enter the next stage, where having somehow responded to provide coverage in the first 24 hours, the story develops and grows larger and more resources need to be organized and brought to the location. In the succeeding days, more and more in the way of resources tends to be poured into the story, and it can become a logistical and financial nightmare to track what equipment has been sent where, and then to identify and control costs. Covering events on major scale is very expensive, and can run into tens of thousands of dollars a day!

Risk to personnel

As we said earlier, 'no story is worth a life', and that has to be the overriding consideration when sending any newsgathering team to cover a story in a hostile environment. If we take that saying to its extreme, the story may not be covered, so it is a matter of the inherent risks being minimized as much as possible. There are some situations where unfortunately the risks are too high, as it has been obvious that in the last decade the media themselves became targets in some conflicts – for example, Chechnya, Kosovo, East Timor and Iraq. In conflicts in previous decades, the presence of the media was generally tolerated – but that cannot any longer be assumed, and is an added factor when trying to assess the risks.

The team

The typical newsgathering team – usually a minimum of reporter, producer, cameraman, video editor, sound technician as well as the uplink operators – all should ideally be equipped to deal with such situations, and strategies worked out to deal with the various possible scenarios.

This might imply that the planning involved in covering a war or civil disturbance is formulaic, but that is unfortunately not so. Nor is there necessarily much time to debate and prepare as much as would be ideal. It is a matter of ensuring that certain steps are taken to ensure, as much as possible, the safety of the team. Circumstances permitting this may include picking team members who have had previous experience of working in war zones, and ideally who have had relevant survival training. At the very least, the planning will include engaging a local fixer – a local civilian contact who can keep abreast of the situation, possibly cultivating military, police and other contacts, and act as translator to the newsgathering team in the field. Any source that can be used to develop an informed knowledge of the situation, including reports from other journalists, all adds to the quality of the planning process, which may also involve discussion with other 'friendly' newsgatherers involved in covering the same story to share hazard assessments.

Train for survival

The hazards faced by the team obviously vary from situation to situation. The reporter, producer, cameraman and sound technician will be working a lot of the time at the 'front line', while the video editor and uplink operators will probably be in a position further away at the 'base' position. Alternatively, the base position may also be liable to attack, and the whole team is equally vulnerable.

Many newsgathering teams have been trained to be able to defend themselves for NBC attacks (nuclear, biological and chemical) in the Persian Gulf and Afghanistan conflicts, and travelled to such areas with appropriate personal protection equipment. Other training that many in the media have undertaken includes battlefield first aid and survival training. The use of flak jackets and helmets, as well as other personal protective equipment, are basic tools nowadays for the well-travelled and well-prepared newsgathering team, and they have usually had some paramilitary training in personal protection. There are a number of specialist companies that sprang up in the 1990s, often run by ex-military special forces personnel, who run short intensive training programmes for media personnel who are going into war zones or other types of hostile environment.

Other equipment that is commonly used are hand-held GPS navigation aids and typically the compact Inmarsat Mini-M satphones. It should be noted that GPS units are position-reporting equipment, and in some conflicts a hostile military force may consider this as espionage equipment if a newsgathering team are caught in possession.

Accepting the risk

Each member of the team should accept the assignment knowing the risks, and ideally a full risk assessment will have been completed to protect personnel. As the overall objective is journalistic, the producer or the reporter will obviously lead the team, but every member of the team has their part to play, and they will be working together in an intense and frightening environment for days or weeks. The whole team is also under considerable pressure to 'make it' on time in terms of transmissions. Reports are often only prepared shortly before the transmission time, as there is always a feeling of having to work 'up to the wire' for the report to contain the very latest information and situation report.

Getting in to the war zone

Having made the decision to try to cover the story, the next problem to be solved is how to get into the conflict zone. Normally, as soon as a country is approaching a war footing, scheduled airline flights are cancelled and civilian airports are closed. It may still be possible to get in by chartered aircraft, although chartering fees are likely to be increased due to the high risks of aircraft either being attacked or being impounded on landing. It is also possible that the situation is so volatile that although there seemed no obstacle on landing, and having dropped off the newsgathering team, by the time the aircraft is ready to take-off, it is not possible.

In recent conflicts, newsgatherers have on occasion been able to 'hitch a ride' with aircraft involved in UN peacekeeping activities in the conflict. This can be difficult, as it may be a matter of waiting until an aircraft is available with enough payload to carry all the equipment.

Since the Gulf conflict in 1990, it has become generally accepted that the electronic media serve a role in publicizing the events in a conflict, and contribute to the overall political process of informing the public. All conflicts have some degree of news reporting from inside the conflict zone, and some media will always find a way in. Nevertheless, it is unlikely that any newsgathering organization will wish to send in a full-size SNG flyaway into a conflict zone where the team has to be able to move quickly and at short notice. Dragging over a tonne of equipment around flies in the face of this, but as we saw earlier when looking at Inmarsat, there are other options to enable newsgatherers deliver breaking news reports.

An interesting facet of the coverage of the conflict in Kosovo is that the deployment of SNG trucks into an area of major international conflict was seen for the first time (in addition to the use of flyaways). Due to the fact that the Balkans are part of Europe, with countries with developed infrastructures on all sides, a significant number of newsgatherers and independent operators were able to get trucks in either overland via Romania, Bulgaria, Hungary, Greece, or by ferry across the Adriatic from Italy. Many of the trucks waited in Albania, Macedonia and Montenegro until the NATO forces were ready to move in, providing coverage of the story, and some were at the vanguard of the push into Kosovo with NATO forces as the Serbian army and militia left. A few trucks were damaged, either by Kosovan Serbs (for revenge), by Serbia on the grounds of no permission to operate having been given (mostly NATO nationality operators), or as the story died down and crews were on the way out, impounded by Macedonia on the grounds of Customs violations. (Several newsgatherers also had flyaway systems damaged or lost in Serbia – either damaged inadvertently in the NATO attacks or again impounded by the authorities.)

Locating the uplink

Having taken an SNG uplink in to a war zone, it needs to be in as safe a position as possible which allows relative ease of access to the news interest.

193

It may be in a hotel, at a government facility, or can even be in a private house rented for the operation. In some situations, all the newsgathering operations are gathered together in one place, in others they are scattered around. From the newsgatherers' point of view, the advantage of the media being together is that they are able to help each other out (as long as it does not interfere with editorial competitiveness), and it also facilitates the sharing of material where such arrangements exist. What determines where the media gather can vary from government 'diktat' to wherever happens to be a natural congregating point.

For instance, during the recent Iraq crises from 1997 to 2003, the media in Iraq were required by the government to be grouped together at the Ministry of Information in Baghdad, and required to stay at a nearby hotel. During the conflict in Bosnia, most of the media in Sarajevo were grouped at the local TV station, not because of any diktat, but because that was a natural congregation point. In the Iraq crisis of 2003, the main centre of media activity was in Doha in Qatar as that was where the US Central Command had facilitated the media to establish their satellite communications.

The uplink is often located on a rooftop or balcony of a building, and it is usually rigged so that in case of attack it can be remotely controlled from inside the building, enabling live transmissions to continue. Inmarsat satphones are also similarly rigged so that communications can be maintained at all times. The advantage of this arrangement has been seen in the Iraqi crises in particular, where live reports from Baghdad have been sustained during air attacks from Coalition aircraft. Of course, the fact that media are gathered in particular locations means that these locations are (hopefully) not targeted.

Plans on how to move the SNG uplink around have to be in hand. During the course of a conflict, it is sometimes necessary to be able to move the SNG uplink to other locations within the zone. This will inevitably be by road, and typically need at least two sturdy four-wheel drive vehicles. The use of the word 'road' here is meant in its loosest sense, and therefore four-wheel drive vehicles are an absolute necessity. However, there may be situations that require greater ingenuity. When the BBC took an SNG flyaway uplink into Afghanistan after the September 11 (2001) attack on the United States, they used pack mules to transport the uplink equipment over the border.

It is almost essential that armour-plated vehicles are used if there is a serious risk of the team coming under fire. This will obviously give a greater degree of protection to the reporter and camera crew as they move around, as well as offering a way of moving the SNG uplink around if required.

It is worth mentioning that the mere possession of armoured vehicles can also make the newsgathering team subject to attack. This is either because they can be mistaken for legitimate targets, or because particularly in a civil war, one or both sides is likely to be short of arms and military equipment, and tempted by such attractive transport available for the taking. The fact that the vehicle is being operated by a news organization is of no consequence.

It would be irresponsible for any news organization not to have carefully laid plans for evacuation of their team in a hostile environment for when the situation deteriorates to absolute danger – this would be part of the risk assessment. Judging the moment when the time is right to pull out is difficult to determine remotely, and detailed discussions with the team usually occur before the decision is taken. Because of the financial (and strategic) value of the SNG uplink, the means of escape usually includes measures to get the uplink out as well.

As with getting the team in, the quickest way of getting people out is generally primarily by air, or as a second choice by road. There will not be any scheduled airline traffic from a war zone, so if it is appropriate to use aircraft as a means of escape, the two usual methods are either by military (often UN) air transport, or by having a chartered aircraft available near at hand. Even if such an arrangement is in place, it is common to have a 'Plan B' for getting personnel and equipment out by road.

Pool arrangements

In some situations, the forming of a media pool either is by mutual consent of the newsgathering organizations, or it is a condition imposed on the media by an external authority. Many of the large news networks have been forced to pool their resources, as the problems of access, transportation, cost and local politics may conspire against them each having their own facilities on the ground. Often these pools are organized on a national or regional basis – for instance, the US networks may form a pool serving US interests, the Japanese networks for their interests, and the EBU may provide facilities for its members. At other times, where strategic alliances exist between certain newsgatherers, joint operations may be established.

A pool formed voluntarily is usually because of overwhelming safety considerations and has occurred particularly once a situation has significantly worsened either because of military action or because of a direct threat of military action against the media. The pool arrangement is likely to involve minimizing the number of personnel on the ground while still providing enough material for the differing news interests. It can also be formed and dissolved in different phases of the conflict, and constantly reviewed. The personnel most exposed are likely to be reporters and camera crews, and the focus will be on providing enough reporting crews to cover the different facets of the conflict. Nevertheless, the number of active SNG uplinks will be kept down to minimize the numbers of personnel in the area. This may involve either withdrawing or mothballing (storing) uplinks for a period until the situation improves.

Where a pool is demanded by an external authority – for instance, by a national government on the grounds of security – the newsgathering organizations will be forced to comply or risk having all their press access withdrawn. Newsgatherers generally comply with these demands, though it has been known for individual 'maverick' operations to be undertaken to try to bypass such restrictions.

Operating SNG uplinks has a number of factors to be considered that go beyond the merely technical, and have a direct impact on the safety of people – both the operators and the public – in a number of different dimensions. The influence on time pressure on covering news events can push the significance of some of these factors into the background unless there is a commitment not to ignore them. International travel with the typical volume of SNG flyaway equipment escalates the stakes, and deploying to a hostile environment pushes the decision-making processes to a very high level of pressure, both in terms of safety and costs.

In the fiercely competitive news everyone in the field wants to be first and 'live' – but above all, they need to be alive.

Logistics

Logistics in the context of newsgathering – and this particularly applies to SNG – can be defined as the science of moving equipment and personnel from A to B in the quickest time at the lowest cost. It is probably the key strategy for success in newsgathering, as there is no merit in having highly skilled staff with the very latest technology if they are not where the story is. Yet the challenge of moving often quite large volumes of equipment even to relatively accessible areas of the world in the shortest time can frustrate even the most experienced newsgatherers.

Various factors have to be weighed up before choosing a particular method of moving both equipment and personnel to a location – and they do not necessarily travel by the same method on pre-planned operations compared to a breaking news story. When covering stories in hostile environments such as war zones, there may not be any choice to be exercised if, for example, facilities for the press are being provided by organizations such as the UN or the military.

Critical factors

There are five fundamental factors to be considered when deploying an SNG uplink to a news story. These are:

(1) the location
(2) how quickly
(3) the costs
(4) the availability of transportation
(5) the availability of space segment.

Although they can be classified neatly into these five areas, there is a complex inter-reaction that means they have to be considered in parallel, rather than in sequence as this list might suggest at first glance. These are also not necessarily the only issues, but they are the ones that have to be considered on all deployments.

Getting to the location is, however, the first factor to be considered. For a local story, the answer is probably perfectly obvious, and an SNG or ENG truck can be sent. The story can be on the air within the hour, and no thought to the process is necessary by the newsroom dispatcher. The location becomes an issue when it is more remote from the broadcasting centre or news agency headquarters.

It is an inevitable truism that many of the world's worst disasters, which involve the natural forces of weather and the earth, tend to occur in regions which are often the most remote and therefore relatively inaccessible. The emergency services and relief agencies struggle to access these areas, and the news media are also in a race to bring the story of the events to the wider world.

Even where the location is in a very highly developed region, the scale of the disaster can completely overwhelm a country's resources. An example of this was the huge earthquake in Kobe, Japan, in 1995, where within a few minutes, 6000 people were killed, 30 000 injured, and over 100 000 buildings were destroyed – and the whole infrastructure of the region was destroyed.

For any newsgathering team to cover these types of event, the problems of the location can dictate how the story is covered. Many of the large news networks have been forced to pool their resources, as the problems of access, transportation, cost and local politics may conspire against them each having their own facilities on the ground. Assuming the location is in another country or continent, the choices facing the newsgatherer in terms of getting the equipment and personnel to the location of the story fall into the category of deciding whether the equipment can be sent by one of the following means:

- on a scheduled flight as excess baggage
- on a scheduled flight as freight
- a specially chartered flight.

Chartering

The fastest and probably the most expensive way of getting to a story is usually on an aircraft chartered especially for the assignment. There is also a potential problem that although a flight may be available at the right time with the required number of seats for the newsgathering team, there is not the aircraft hold capacity to take an SNG flyaway, which can take a significant amount of baggage space.

But on the other hand, a charter may not be so expensive if the story is significant enough that other press organizations are willing to share the cost for space on the flight. This may, in fact, turn out to be the cheapest option for all parties if the aircraft is large enough to get everyone (reporters, producers and technicians) and their equipment on board – and that includes camera and editing equipment as well as the SNG uplink.

Excess baggage

For stories of lesser significance, the fastest method, after chartering, is to travel on a scheduled flight with the equipment carried as excess baggage. Bearing in mind the typical weight of an SNG flyaway is in excess of a tonne, and excess baggage rates are typically 1% per kilo of the single first class passenger fare on long-haul flights, the bill could run into tens of thousands of dollars. This is for just a one-way trip, and will probably exceed the cost of the airline seats for the news team by a significant factor. However, many large newsgathering organizations have negotiated special bulk rate deals with a number of carriers, and this rate can drop significantly if such a deal is in place.

Freighting

The third option is to air freight the equipment. This is an option where the operation can be pre-planned where it is to cover a known event (such as an international conference or national elections). It is also an option at the end of a major news story where the equipment can be brought back at a more leisurely pace.

The process of freighting equipment is more involved because of the Customs procedures at the point of departure and at the destination. On arrival at the destination, the equipment similarly has to be handled by the destination shipping agent, which will arrange for clearance through Customs. The time taken at each end to process the shipment can be between two days to over a week! Allowing for flight time, it may take over a week to air freight equipment to a destination, even though it may only be on a flight of less than 24 hours – considerably longer than the actual travel time. This is of course a significant factor to take into account for this is 'dead' time for the equipment. Once it has embarked on this route, it is virtually irretrievable if it is suddenly required for another story. The advantage of course is the costs, which are likely to be a fraction of excess baggage costs.

Carriage of systems on aircraft

No matter how the equipment is going to be transported, it has to be packaged correctly for travel, and we looked at the packaging of flyaway systems earlier. The industry body that deals with international civil aviation is the International Air Transport Association (IATA). It establishes the regulations and standards for safe international air transport, and its membership is made up of all the international air carriers. One of the areas it regulates is how and what goods are carried, and SNG flyaway systems are treated no differently to any other type of cargo. The flyaway flight cases have to be within certain dimensions, as covered by the IATA rules on the dimensions of packaging cases, and of course have to be rugged enough to withstand the rigours of international air transport.

One of the items typically carried as part of an SNG flyaway system is a petrol generator for powering the system. Unfortunately, it is a difficult piece of equipment to transport by air, as it is classed as dangerous goods. The IATA has regulations that cover the carriage of all hazardous goods, and this includes petrol generators – a petrol generator is essentially a petrol engine driving a small electrical generator. In the packing and transportation of generators of this type, it requires that the fuel tank and the fuel system be completely drained. Failure to comply with this requirement will result in the generator not being loaded onto the aircraft. In practice, many carriers are not keen to carry petrol-engined generators, even if all the precautions have been taken.

Of course, there is the option to try and hire or buy generators locally on arrival, but this leaves too much to chance. The availability of generators, particularly in a disaster zone or a hostile environment, is likely to be poor and much time can be wasted trying to source a generator while stories can not be transmitted.

The generator is not the most obvious component in a flyaway system yet it is very essential to most overseas SNG flyaway operations to provide flexibility. It is also the one item that has been left behind on the airport tarmac on more occasions than most newsgathering teams care to remember.

Logistics

Loading SNG equipment onto an aircraft in Africa (courtesy Paul Szeless)

On the horizon

It may seem odd that the use of SNG has not completely superseded the use of ENG terrestrial microwave in trucks, but the bare facts are that for many locations in metropolitan areas, terrestrial microwave still has an advantage over the use of satellites. Nevertheless, the spread of SNG continues, and the future probably lies in the use of hybrid vehicles to an increasing degree.

Much has been written and spoken of over the last few years of the impact of the Internet on all aspects of our lives – and newsgathering is no exception. However, while it has become common to send prepared stories as a file in Store and Forward mode either via an Inmarsat satphone or even a convenient cybercafe, the use of full size SNG terminals will continue.

Just recently we have seen several manufacturers offer very compact terminals, which offer digitally compressed data rates from 600 kbps to 8 Mbps.

Some of these new systems offer an IP connection, which makes the uplink equipment adaptable to new ways of transmitting video and audio material.

The recent conflict in Iraq saw some innovative use of new SNG technology, and there is no doubt that we will continue to see a reduction in the size, weight and price of the equipment, matched by an increase in user-friendliness, functionality and flexibility.

Glossary of terms

4:2:0	digital video signal chrominance sampling standard
4:2:2	digital video signal chrominance sampling standard – twice that of 4:2:0
4-wire	studio communication with separate send and return circuits enabling simultaneous bi-directional (two-way) conversations
601	digital video standard (CCIR 601)
acquiring the bird	locating the satellite
AGC	automatic gain control
AM	amplitude modulation
amplitude modulation	a baseband message signal modulates (alters) the amplitude and frequency of a high frequency carrier signal at a nominally fixed frequency, so that the intensity, or amplitude, of the carrier wave varies in accordance with the modulating signal
amplitude	magnitude
analogue	signal which can take on a continuous range of values between a minimum and a maximum value; method of transmitting information by continuously variable quantities, as opposed to digital transmission, which is characterized by discrete 'bits' of information in numerical steps
Apstar	Asia-Pacific region satellite system
Arabsat	Middle Eastern satellite system
artefacts	faults seen in a digital video picture
ASI	Asynchronous Standard Interface – a digital connection standard
AsiaSat	Asia-Pacific region satellite system
auditory masking	where parts of an audio signal not discernible by the human ear can be imperceptibly removed – method of fooling the human brain into hearing what is not present
automatic gain control	method of automatically compensating for varying levels in a signal
auto-tracking	system used on an antenna to automatically follow the target satellite signal
baseband	refers to audio and video signals
bays	equipment cabinets
beacon	identification signal transmitted by a satellite
beam coverage	area of coverage of a particular satellite transponder
belt-pack	compact comms unit worn on a waist belt
BER	bit error rate
bird	satellite

bit error rate	indication of digital signal quality
bit	the smallest element of a binary number – '0' or '1'
bit rate	speed of data transmission, measured in bits per second
bits per second	measure of speed of data transmission
black line flashing	transmission error seen on analogue trans-mitted pictures
blimp	airship
blockiness	see pixellation
boresight	strongest focussed signal emitted from a microwave (satellite or terrestrial) antenna
bounce signal	signal path achieved by reflecting signals off buildings, large objects, etc.
bps	bits per second
breaking story	refers to a news story in its beginning phase
bring down	finish a satellite transmission
bring up	start a satellite transmission
broadbeam	type of satellite beam; spotbeam
CA	conditional access
capture	process of converting video and audio signals into a digital format for manipulation on a PC
carrier signal	the base signal on which information is modulated, either in amplitude, frequency or phase
C-band	refers to the 4–6 GHz frequency band centre frequency
chain	a set of equipment for transmission or reception
channel	refers to a transmission channel in a micro-wave link frequency band or on a satellite transponder
check bits	to enable error correction, added to the bit stream in a modulator to enable errors to be detected at the downlink
chrominance	colour signal
clean carrier	unmodulated carrier
cleanfeed	see return audio
clear	command from the studio that the remote contribution is complete
cliff-edge	characteristic of decoded digital signal – either it is completely present or absent
coded orthogonal frequency division multiplex	(COFDM) method of digitally transmitting a terrestrial microwave signal using a large number of narrow information carriers – typically at least 2000 – each carrying a slice of the total compressed data

COFDM	coded orthogonal frequency division multiplex
collecting area	describes the area of a receiving antenna that has a clear unobstructed view towards the satellite or other microwave transmitter
colour difference	in an analogue television signal, the technique of embedding the colour information in along with the luminance signal
comms	communications (with the studio)
commslink	system of using two separate narrow bandwidth digital satellite carriers to provide bi-directional studio communications
composite	analogue TV signal that is transmitted combining the luminance, colour and timing signals into one combined signal
compressed	the process of digital compression
compression	the digital process by which redundant information can be removed from video and audio signals without the viewer perceiving the loss of information
conditional access	digital encryption system used to protect unauthorized viewing of the programme
contribution	the process of feeding material to a studio for transmission
cross-polar discrimination	the property of a receive antenna to reject signals on the opposite polarization so that any interference from a signal on the same frequency but opposite polarization is minimized
crosstalk	interference between different but adjacent signals
cue	signal to begin speaking on air
cut, cut-piece	an edited story
cutting together	editing a story from raw material (rushes)
dangerous goods	IATA definition of goods considered hazardous for carriage on commercial aircraft
dB	decibel
dBi	unit of measurement of gain of an antenna
decibel	(dB) – expression of ratios of two power levels in logarithmic form
decoder	a device that decodes a compressed MPEG-2 video and audio signal stream
dedicated capacity	capacity on a satellite that has been specifically set aside for a particular purpose
demodulation, demodulator	the process of recovering information from a modulated signal, using a demodulator
DENG	Digital ENG
desk	control console, typically audio mixer

digital ENG	typically refers to COFDM digital microwave transmission
direct-to-home	satellite distribution of programmes directly to the consumer via a dish on the viewers home
difference signals	see colour difference; the colour elements in a composite TV signal
digital	information expressed as data for transmission; signal state expressed as on (1) and off (0) states; a binary signal
dish	colloquial term for a satellite antenna; also generic term for an SNG uplink operation
distribution	the process of distributing signals via a terrestrial or satellite network to audiences
down-the-line	a two-way interview between the presenter in the studio, and the reporter or a guest on location
downconverter	unit for translating frequencies from one frequency band down to another
drive	term used for the low power signal applied to the input of a high power amplifier
dropouts	picture flashing and rolling due to disturbances in the received signal
DTH	direct-to-home
dual purpose	vehicles that have both a satellite uplink and a terrestrial microwave link – see hybrid
dual band	refers to equipment that covers both C and Ku frequency bands
ducting	effect where radio signal paths are altered due to atmospheric effects; see also layering
dumping	process of allowing air to rapidly escape from a pneumatic mast, hence allowing it to descend much more quickly
DVB compliant; DVB standard	complies to the digital video broadcasting standard
Eb/No	measurement of quality of the received digital signal
effective aperture	area of the antenna that contributes to receiving a signal
effects	normal background sound; see natural sound
electromagnetic interference	interference due to electromagnetic fields, both natural and artificial
electromagnetic spectrum	the range of frequencies from nothing to light
embedded	refers to where a journalist is placed within a military unit at or near the front line of a conflict
EMI	electromagnetic interference

encoder	device that translates baseband video and audio signals into a compressed signal
end of life	final stage of a satellite's life before it is taken out of service
end-fire antenna	a helix or rod antenna used in terrestrial ENG microwave, and is circularly polarized
ENG	electronic news gathering
error correction	process of adding data in transmission to improve reliability of recovering received decoded data
Eurobeam	particular type of beam shaped to cover the European continent
Europe*Star	European satellite system
fade margin	difference between the calculated or actual performance of a link and the threshold of operation
feed	a circuit providing a supplementary element e.g. return audio from the studio; to send an edited package over a link
feed arm	on an antenna, the arm which holds the feedhorn at the correct distance from the focus of the parabola
feedhorn; feed	device which emits the microwave signal
field	describes part of the television signal, where there are 2 fields to every frame, and 50/60 fields per second depending on the TV standard
firewire	standard cable for connecting DV camcorders to PCs
fixer	someone who has a good deal of local knowledge, and be able to 'fix' things from finding and making the contacts to make sure the whole operation runs as smoothly as possible. May also act as local translator
flange	term for the opening or port on the feed or on the output of a high power amplifier
flown	where cables are suspended above ground level for safety and logistical reasons
flux-gate	type of sophisticated and accurate electromagnetic compass
flyaway	boxed transportable SNG terminal
FM	frequency modulation
focus	on a parabolic antenna, the point at which the signal is at its maximum
footprint	term for the coverage of a satellite transponder
forward error correction	data correction signal added at the uplink to enhance concealment of errors that occur on the passage of the signal via the satellite to the downlink
fps	frames per second

frame	two fields of a television signal
frames per second	speed of display of the television picture
frequency	period of cycle of a signal, measured in Hertz (Hz)
frequency modulation	process whereby a carrier signal is shifted up and down in frequency from its centre frequency in direct relationship to the amplitude of the baseband signal
Fresnel zones	in terrestrial microwave, the group of zones in which there should not be any obstruction, as it is likely that a reflection will cause an 'opposing' signal to be bounced off the obstruction – only the first Fresnel zone is of significance
full-time	type of satellite transponder lease
gain	refers to the magnification factor of signal
Galaxy	US satellite system, part of PanAmSat
gallery	production and technical control rooms of TV station
geostationary	where an object such as a satellite appears motionless above the earth
geostationary arc	grouping of satellites that sit in a circular orbit above the Equator at a distance of 35 785 km above the Earth's surface at any point on the Equator
geostationary orbit	describes the orbit of a satellite in the geostationary arc
get-away	slang term for look angle
ghosting	effect seen on TV pictures where the received analogue signal is made up of both direct line and reflected signals
global	type of C-band satellite transponder beam
go live	the process of carrying out a live transmission
golden rod	see end-fire antenna
goodnight	agreed time between the SNG operator and the satellite control centre for the end of transmission
guard interval; guard band	space allowed in frequency to protect adjacent channels
GVs	general views – pictures shot of the environs of a story to add to the editing of the story
hands back	where the reporter finishes a live transmission
hazard	anything that can cause harm
head load	term for the total package of equipment at the top of a pneumatic mast
head unit	in terrestrial microwave, generic term for the power amplifier and associated equipment at the top of a pneumatic mast; in SNG, the feedhorn
head-end	cable TV distribution point for an area

Glossary

heading	direction in which the antenna is pointing
helix antenna	see end-fire antenna
hemi	type of C-band satellite transponder beam
Hertz	unit of measurement of frequency
high power amplifier	used in both terrestrial microwave and SNG, the unit that boosts the low power signal up to high power for delivery via the antenna
Hispasat	European satellite system
hop	a single leg of a microwave link path
hostile environment	term describing an area which is suffering civil or military conflict – from a riot to a war
hot-spare	spare equipment connected and powered, ready for instant use in the event of failure of the main equipment
hot spots	areas on a flexible waveguide where there are RF burns
HPA	high power amplifier
HSD	high speed data – Inmarsat term
hub-mount	where the HPA is mounted directly onto the antenna, rather than some distance way and connected by a length of waveguide
hybrid	vehicles that have both a satellite uplink and a terrestrial microwave link – see dual-purpose
Hz	Hertz – unit of measurement of frequency
ident	video or audio signal played out on a circuit to identify the source e.g. location
IF	intermediate frequency
IFB	interrupted fold back
illuminate	term describing the flooding of the parabolic antenna with microwave signal – either in transmit or receive
inclined orbit	satellite status near end of its operational life, though this type of capacity is often used for SNG
information	term for the video and/or audio signal that is to be conveyed
interlaced	in a television frame of two TV fields, where each TV field is offset by a line, and each pair of TV fields is sent in alternate sequence of odd- and even-numbered lines in the field
intermediate frequency	signal between stages in an uplink or downlink transmission chain – typically at frequencies of 70 or 140 MHz, or in the L-band (at around 1000 MHz or 1 GHz)
International Telecommunications Union	global body that decides on radio frequency usage

interrupted fold back	a mix of the studio output without the audio contribution from the remote location but with talkback from the studio gallery superimposed on top
interview mode	see low delay mode
investigation levels	NRPB definition for non-ionizing radiation, levels below which adverse biological effects are likely to occur
ITU	International Telecommunications Union
JCSAT	Asia-Pacific satellite system
Ku-band	frequency range from 10.5 to 17 GHz; in SNG, the frequency band 14.0–14.50 GHz for transmission, and 10.7–12.75 GHz for reception
laptop editor	portable editing system utilizing two VTR decks with two screens and control software
latency	delay through a compression process
launcher	slang term for feedhorn
layering	effect where radio signal paths are altered due to atmospheric effects; see also ducting
levels	see main level; main profile
LHCP	left hand circular polarization
licence	legal document authorizing transmission, issued by government department
line of sight	required to achieve clear transmission; an uninterrupted path between the transmitting antenna and the receiving antenna
lines	method by which a TV frame is divided up into tiny horizontal strips
line-up	the period immediately prior to a programme transmission when test signals are transmitted and parameters checked to ensure the transmission is of the highest quality
link	generic term for the connection between a remote location and the studio via terrestrial microwave or satellite
link budget	theoretical calculation for assessing whether a terrestrial or microwave or satellite link will work
'live'	the process of a live transmission
live end	slang term for the camera position connected to an ENG microwave truck or an SNG uplink
live two-way	where the viewer sees a presentation of the story, switching between the studio and the location, including interaction with the reporter at the scene
live updates	regular live two-ways keeping the viewer abreast of the enfolding story
lobe	element of the radiation pattern of an antenna
look angle	describes the unobstructed visual path required for a terrestrial microwave or satellite link for successful transmission

Glossary

209

low delay mode	MPEG-2 encoder mode that offers the facility to improve the latency at the expense of movement compensation, reducing the overall processing time of the signal
luminance	the parameter of a TV picture which describes its brightness
main level; main profile	types of MPEG-2 service
man-pack links	small and light battery-powered terrestrial microwave transmitter packs usually mounted onto a backpack, with the antenna projecting above the head of the operator
master control room	TV station technical control centre
matrixing	process by which colour systems derive a composite luminance signal from mixing the red, blue and green signals, producing colour difference signals
matting	covering of cables with heavy-duty rubber matting in streets and areas of public access to minimize trip hazard
MCR	master control room
meridians	imaginary symmetrical lines of reference that run from the North to the South Poles and are called lines of longitude
microwave repeater	see mid-point
mid-point	a terrestrial microwave repeater that receives and retransmits the signal on to the next point in the chain
mix-minus	a mix of the studio output without the audio contribution from the remote location; see also cleanfeed, interrupted fold back, reverse audio and return audio
modulation; modulator	the process of inserting information into a transmitted carrier signal, using a modulator
MPEG	Motion Pictures Expert Group
MPEG-2	standard covering the compression, encoding and decoding of video and audio data for digital television
mothballing	storage of equipment at a remote location in preparation for the next event
MSps	mega symbols per second
multilateral	point-to-multipoint contribution
multipath	interference from reflected signals
multiplex; multiplexing	process of combining two or more programme digital streams to provide a single digital data stream to the uplink chain

multi-skilling	where technicians, operators and journalists are trained in at least one (and often two) other crafts apart from their primary core skill
Nahuelsat	Pan-American satellite system
NBC	nuclear, biological and chemical
natural sound	normal background sound; see effects
Nilesat	North African satellite system
No Story Is Worth A Life	mantra of every operator on location
noise	unwanted signal
non-dedicated	type of satellite capacity
NTSC	National Television Standards Committee; US analogue TV standard
Nycoil	brand of brightly coloured polyurethane air-brake hose used for carrying cables up a pneumatic mast
OB	outside broadcast
occasional	type of satellite capacity
off-air	TV programme signal received at the location by terrestrial or satellite reception
offset prime focus	type of SNG uplink antenna
on-line	term for editing VTRs connected directly to the terrestrial microwave or SNG uplink system
optimized	term for the accurate pointing of the terrestrial microwave or SNG uplink antenna
oscilloscope	measurement instrument for displaying signals
out-words	the last half a dozen words at the end of an edited piece which prepare the studio presenter or reporter to pick up the story
over-run	in satellite transmissions, state where the transmission has run beyond the booked end time
package	edited story
packet identifier	MPEG-2 channel identifier containing all the navigation information required to identify and reconstruct a programme stream
PAL	Phase Alternate Line; principally European analogue TV standard
panned-up	term to describe when the terrestrial microwave transmit and receive antennas are correctly aligned to each other
parabolic; paraboloid	mathematical term for the typical shape of a terrestrial microwave or SNG uplink dish
parallels	lines of latitude
path	generic term for the connection between two points of a link; in MPEG-2 transmission, a term for a programme stream
path profile	report generated from topographical map information based on the location of the TX and RX

Glossary

211

	points, which will be translated into a cross-section of the land underneath the signal path
peak-to-peak	the maximum distance between upper and lower points of a signal
perceptual compression	process of compression that 'tricks' the brain into thinking that the material looks and sounds like the original
permission	temporary agreement by a foreign government allowing the importation and operation of an SNG uplink
personal protection badges	small badges worn on the body to warn of excessive non-ionizing radiation levels
petals	segments of an SNG antenna reflector
phase-combiner	SNG system where two or more chains are combined to feed via a single antenna
picture element	see pixel
PID	packet identifier
piece-to-camera	where the reporter stands at a strategic point against a background which sets the scene for the story and recounts the events directly to the camera
pixel	smallest perceptible block of picture (an abbreviation of 'picture element')
pixellation	a particular type of digital artefact, where picture elements coalesce momentarily into rectangular areas of picture with distinct boundaries (also referred to as 'blockiness')
plumbing	slang term for the microwave waveguide interconnections
pneumatic mast	a series of hollow telescopic tube sections each extended by pumping compressed air into the mast base, pushing each of the sections up
polarization	refers to the geometric plane in which the electromagnetic waves are transmitted or received; describing the orientation of the electric field radiated from the antenna
polarization skew	rotation of the feedhorn to compensate for the angular difference between the antenna position on the Earth's surface and the satellite position
pool	where a group of newsgatherers agree to share pictures and/or resources on a story for common use
prime focus antenna	type of SNG uplink antenna
profiles	see main level; main profile
PTC	piece-to-camera
rack	equipment cabinet
Rack Unit	internationally recognized way of measuring the height and width of equipment – width is defined

	as 19 inches, and 1 RU is equal to 1.75 inches (44.5 mm) high
radio	electromagnetic radiation
radio-cam	a compact low-power short-range microwave link mounted on the camera, powered from the camera battery
range patterns	frequency test patterns of the performance of the antenna measured on a test range, defining the performance of the antenna
rate card	a standard published price listing for services or facilities, often used as the basis for negotiation
RCD	residual current device
real time	the actual running time
receive frequency	specific centre frequency of the reception channel
redundancy	unnecessary information in an uncompressed signal; a second set of equipment to provide back-up in the event of failure
Reed–Solomon	a method of error correction where each block of data of programme signal has an additional check block of data added to compensate for any errors that the signal may suffer on its passage from the transmitter to the receiver
reflection	a signal that has taken a non-direct path, causing a slightly time-delayed replica of the direct path signal to be received that can (usually) adversely affect the overall link performance
reflector	the transmitting/receiving surface of a parabolic antenna
residual current device	a safety device that monitors the power supply constantly checking for a fault condition
resolution	sharpness
return audio	a mix of the studio output without the audio contribution from the remote location
return video	video feed either from the studio to the remote location, and/or from the ENG/SNG truck to the camera
reverse audio	see return audio
reverse talkback	remote location-to-studio talkback
reverse video	see return video
RF	radio frequency
RHCP	right hand circularly polarized
risk	the chance, whether high or low, that somebody will be harmed by a hazard
rod antenna	helix or end-fire antenna used in terrestrial ENG microwave
RU	Rack Unit

running order	list generated for a news bulletin showing order and timings of stories
rushes	raw unedited shot footage
RX	receive
safety zone	area cordoned off in front of a terrestrial microwave or SNG antenna to prevent the risk of exposure to high levels of non-ionizing radiation
sample	an instantaneous measured value of an analogue signal
satellite telephone	typically an Inmarsat terminal that enables voice or high-speed data connections from remote locations
satphone	slang term for satellite telephone
SDI	serial digital interface
security key	used in conditional access systems to protect content
SHF	super high frequency
shooting	colloquial term for the transmission of a microwave signal
side lobes	see lobe
site survey; site test	a test carried out to see if a link will work prior to the actual event
SNG	satellite news gathering
SNV	satellite newsgathering vehicle
Solidaridad	South American satellite system
space segment	that part of the signal path between the satellite uplink and downlink
spatial redundancy	the removal of redundant information carried out in two dimensions within each frame of picture
spectral redundancy	the removal of redundant information carried out between colour values at any one point in the picture
spectrum analyser	measurement instrument for displaying signal frequencies across a spectrum
stabilizers	retractable legs fitted so that the inevitable rock in a vehicle's suspension is minimized
starter link	the originating link in a terrestrial microwave link path
stand-up	term for a camera position and shot as a backdrop to enable a reporter to convey the sense of the story for straightforward pieces-to-camera
sub-carrier	an extra narrow FM audio carrier that is mixed with the main FM video carrier signal
SUV	sports utility vehicle
switched talkback	talkback from the studio gallery that is only active when the studio wish to speak to the remote location (as opposed to open talkback, which allows the remote location to hear everything going on in the studio gallery)
synchronously switch	switch between video sources with no picture roll or glitch

talent	the reporter or correspondent who stands in front of the camera
talkback	communication circuit between the studio gallery and the remote location that carries purely technical conversations
talked-in	the process of the MCR operator guiding the ENG microwave operator to achieve best signal quality
Telecom	European satellite system
teleport	a downlink facility, usually consisting of a number of antennas pointing at different satellites and connected to a network for interconnecting with TV stations
temporal redundancy	the removal of redundant information carried out between one frame of picture and the next frame usually due to lack of movement
TES	transportable earth station
Thor	European satellite system
thread	commonly used term to describe mode of operation in terms of RF system on an SNG uplink e.g. single thread is a single RF path; dual thread is two RF signal paths
topography	the detailed description of the surfaces of the land
track	the voice commentary from the reporter
traffic	refers to the number of active signals on a satellite
transceiver	*transmitter/receiver*
transmission chain	the complete equipment path between source and destination
transmit frequency	specific centre frequency of the transmission channel
transponder	group of satellite channels
transport stream	MPEG-2 programme stream
transportable earth station	portable satellite uplink e.g. SNG uplink
travelling wave tube	power amplifying device used in an HPA
TS	transport stream
Turksat	Eurasian satellite system
two-way	transmission where the studio and the remote location have an on-air dialogue to inform the audience
TX	transmission
unilateral	point-to-point contribution
upconverter	unit for translating frequencies from one band up to another
uplink	transportable satellite earth station

Glossary

video journalist	a reporter who can also edit tape and/or shoot video and sound
Viterbi	the process of decoding forward error correction in the decoder
VJ	video journalist
VTR	video tape recorder
W	Watts
Watt	unit of measurement of power
waveform	signal shape
waveguide	a specially formed hollow metal tube, usually rectangular in shape in cross section, used to connect the HPA to the antenna
wavelength	a specific frequency in the spectrum
widebeam	type of Ku-band satellite beam
Z	transmission start time

Focal Press

www.focalpress.com

Join Focal Press on-line
As a member you will enjoy the following benefits:

- an email bulletin with **information on new books**
- a regular **Focal Press Newsletter**:
    - featuring a selection of new titles
    - keeps you informed of **special offers, discounts and freebies**
    - alerts you to **Focal Press news and events** such as author signings and seminars
- complete access to **free content** and reference material on the focalpress site, such as the focalXtra articles and commentary from our authors
- a **Sneak Preview** of selected titles (sample chapters) *before* they publish
- a chance to have your say on our **discussion boards** and **review books** for other Focal readers

Focal Club Members are invited to give us feedback on our products and services. Email: worldmarketing@focalpress.com – we want to hear your views!

Membership is **FREE**. To join, visit our website and register. If you require any further information regarding the on-line club please contact:

Lucy Lomas-Walker
Email: l.lomas@elsevier.com
Tel: +44 (0) 1865 314438
Fax: +44 (0) 1865 314572
Address: Focal Press, Linacre House,
Jordan Hill, Oxford, UK, OX2 8DP

Catalogue

For information on all Focal Press titles, our full catalogue is available online at www.focalpress.com and all titles can be purchased here via secure online ordering, or contact us for a free printed version:

USA
Email: christine.degon@bhusa.com
Tel: +1 781 904 2607 T

Europe and rest of world
Email: j.blackford@elsevier.com
Tel: +44 (0) 1865 314220

Potential authors
If you have an idea for a book, please get in touch:

USA
editors@focalpress.com

Europe and rest of world
focal.press@repp.co.uk

Printed in the United Kingdom by
Lightning Source UK Ltd., Milton Keynes
139487UK00001BA/26/P

9 780240 516622